SHAKESPEARE'S FRIENDS

SHAKESPEARE'S FRIENDS

Kate Emery Pogue

PRAEGER

Westport, Connecticut
London

Library of Congress Cataloging-in-Publication Data

Pogue, Kate.
　Shakespeare's friends / Kate Emery Pogue.
　　　p.　cm.
　Includes bibliographical references and index.
　ISBN 0–275–98956–9 (alk. paper)
1. Shakespeare, William, 1564–1616—Friends and associates.　2. Great Britain—
History—Elizabeth, 1558–1603—Biography.　3. Dramatists, English—Early
modern, 1500–1700—Biography.　4. Stratford-upon-Avon (England)—
Biography.　5. London (England)—Biography.　I. Title.
　PR2894.P57　2006
　822.3'3—dc22　　　　2005020950

British Library Cataloguing in Publication Data is available.

Library of Congress Catalog Card Number: 2005020950
ISBN: 0–275–98956–9

First published in 2006

Praeger Publishers, 88 Post Road West, Westport, CT 06881
An imprint of Greenwood Publishing Group, Inc.
www.praeger.com

Printed in the United States of America

The paper used in this book complies with the
Permanent Paper Standard issued by the National
Information Standards Organization (Z39.48–1984).

10 9 8 7 6 5 4 3 2 1

To

Mary B. Scott
Student, Research Assistant, Friend

And to all who consider themselves
Shakespeare's friends

Contents

+==+ +==+

Preface   xi

Introduction   xv

William Shakespeare   1

Shakespeare's Stratford Friends   9

Richard Quiney   13
Hamnet Sadler   17
Richard Tyler   20
Richard Field   22
The Combe Family   27
The Nash Family   30
William Reynolds   31
Thomas Greene   32
John Hall   34
Thomas Russell   38
Alexander Aspinall   40

Julius Shaw   41
John Robinson   42
Francis Collins   43
William Walker   45

Shakespeare's London Friends   47

Friends of a Sort: Shakespeare and Royalty   48
Queen Elizabeth I   50
King James I   53
Henry Wriothesley, the Earl of Southampton   55
Emilia Bassano Lanier   63
The Earls and the Countess of Pembroke   66
Lady Warwick   71
Maria Mountjoy   73
William Johnson   75
Michael Drayton   77
The Davenant Family   80

Friends at Work   83

Philip Henslowe   83
Edward Alleyn   85
Christopher Marlowe   89
Ben Jonson   93
The Collaborators   100
Thomas Dekker   101
Beaumont and Fletcher   104
Francis Beaumont   105
John Fletcher   106
Shareholders and Housekeepers   109
Thomas Pope   111
William Sly   112
Cuthbert Burbage   113
Will Kempe   116

Augustine Phillips   119

Richard Burbage   122

John Heminges   129

Henry Condell   131

The Wives   132

In Stratford: Judith Sadler, Bess Quiney,
Anne Digges Russell, Ann Shaw Aspinall   132

In London: Jacqueline Vautrollier Field, Rebecca
Heminges, Elizabeth Condell, Winifred Burbage   132

The First Folio   137

Conclusion   143

Appendix A: Friendship in Shakespeare's Plays   147

*Appendix B: What Shakespeare's Contemporaries
Said about Him*   153

*Appendix C: Most Important Elizabethan/
Jacobean Dramatists and Actors*   159

*Appendix D: Revisiting Baldwin: Roles the
Friends Played*   161

Notes   165

Selected Bibliography   173

Index   177

Preface

+≒ ≒+

The genesis of this book was a seminar I was asked to give in
Palo Alto, California, on Shakespeare and friendship. Inspired
by the idea, I assumed that material on Shakespeare's many friends
would be readily available. However, nowhere could I find a single
source of gathered information about Shakespeare's close acquaintances. Instead, I had to search through many different, often ob-
scure, sources to ferret out the needed information. I returned to
those sources with pleasure in quest of details for the biographies in
this book.

Among them, Samuel Schoenbaum's *William Shakespeare, A Compact Documentary Life* (Oxford University Press, 1987) remained open
on my desk to keep me in touch with primary sources, and his *Shakespeare's Lives* (Oxford University Press, 1991) served as a constant
reminder that any biographical work is both a biography of the
subject and an autobiography of the author.

E. K. Chambers's classic *William Shakespeare, A Study of Facts and
Problems* (Clarendon, 1930) offered a quantity of primary source material, while the standard twentieth-century biographies—Marchette
Chute's *Shakespeare of London* (Dutton, 1949), Ian Wilson's *Shakespeare, The Evidence* (St. Martin's, 1993), Park Honan's *Shakespeare, A*

Life (Oxford University Press, 1998), F. E. Halliday's *Shakespeare* (Thames and Hudson, 1998), Peter Quennell's *Shakespeare, A Biography* (World, 1963), Robert Payne's *By Me, William Shakespeare* (Everest House, 1980), Anthony Burgess's *Shakespeare* (Penguin, 1972), and A. L. Rowse's *William Shakespeare, A Biography* (Harper & Row, 1963)—illuminated those primary sources with provocative, if sometimes conflicting, interpretations. Stephen Greenblatt's *Will in the World* (Norton, 2004) affirmed the idea that we can learn about a personality by looking at the world in which he lives.

Perhaps the most fun to read, and in some cases reread, were the passionate specialty works: Caroline Spurgeon's *Shakespeare's Imagery, and What It Tells Us* (Cambridge University Press, 1966), Edgar Fripp's *Master Richard Quyny* (Oxford University Press, 1924), C. C. Stopes's *Shakespeare's Warwickshire Contemporaries* (Shakespeare Head, 1907), Robert Giroux's *The Book Known as Q* (Vintage Books, 1982), and Charles Connell's *They Gave Us Shakespeare* (Oriel, 1982), a book that pays homage to Shakespeare's friends Henry Condell and John Heminges, who were the first to publish the complete and accurate version of his plays.

Invaluable for pure fact-checking were F. E. Halliday's *A Shakespeare Companion 1564–1964* (Penguin, 1964), Charles Boyce's *Shakespeare A to Z* (Roundtable, 1990), and Alan and Veronica Palmer's *Who's Who in Shakespeare's England* (St. Martin's, 1999).

Many of the favorite anecdotes about Shakespeare—such as his doggerel verse-writing for Alexander Aspinall's gift of gloves, the epitaph for John Combe, or his drinking bout with Ben Jonson and Michael Drayton just before his death—originated in the late-seventeenth-century and early-eighteenth-century biographical notes of Richard Davies, Thomas Fuller, John Ward, John Aubrey, and Nicholas Rowe. These were the first men to write down what they knew of Shakespeare's life; much that they report is based on unsubstantiated tradition and hearsay. Only the charm of these anecdotes, and our knowledge that they come from the sources closest to Shakespeare's time, recommend them and account for their persistence. In alluding to them, I have tried to acknowledge their existence but also indicate their lack of factual basis. I have kept them because of their pervasiveness in the source material, and because I, too, am subject to their charm.

Unless otherwise noted, quotes from the Shakespeare plays are from *The Complete Works of William Shakespeare*, text established by John Dover Wilson for the Cambridge University Press, 1980.

Organization

Shakespeare's Friends can be read in two ways. It can be used as a reference tool for those researching one or another of the friends out of context with the others. Or it can be read through as a connected narrative. The first section deals with the friends of Shakespeare's childhood and is organized from the older of the friends (Richard Quiney) to the youngest (Richard Tyler). This organization is parallel to the amount of information known concerning each—we know more about Richard Quiney and Richard Field than about Hamnet Sadler. Least is known about Richard Tyler. The Stratford friendships of his middle age and retirement follow those of his childhood.

When Shakespeare goes to London, the biographies begin with Queen Elizabeth I and King James I, as they were the figures that dominated and shaped the society of the age. The acquaintances move downward through the class system, the aristocratic friendships first, then the domestic, ending with Shakespeare's working colleagues. The wives were for the most part dependant on the men they married for their friendship to Shakespeare, and as all too little is known about them, it seemed logical to group them together at the end.

The First Folio reveals the depth of friendship felt for Shakespeare by his friends John Heminges and Henry Condell. The story of their visit to Stratford in 1622 brings us full circle, his London friends coming at last to Shakespeare's final resting place in Stratford.

Acknowledgments

I thank Mary B. Scott, research assistant; Dick Simpson and Sarajane Avidon for their generous advice and support; Scott Andrew Mandel for his faith in the book and professionalism in its marketing; Sidney Berger for suggestions and corrections to the content of the manuscript; Kathleen VanderMeer for invaluable editorial help; Pat Lamb, Elva Stewart, Denise LeBrun, Ann Christensen, and Hilary Mackie, for feedback; Bill Pogue for encouragement and constant help with the recalcitrant computer; Jerilyn Watson and Mike McClory for proofreading and editing advice; Donna Pinnick for rescue from computer scanning dilemmas; Howard Ayers and Jonathan Emery for insights into questions of the Globe and Blackfriars' corporate structures; Mo Sanders for booking the lecture that gave birth to the book idea; Ray and Jane Stedman for their hospitality and help with Shakespeare's connection with the Pembroke family at

Wilton House; Pat Laing David Yarham and Jill and Robin Lunn in England, and James Dick and the staff at Festival Hill, Round Top, Texas, for their help and support; Joan Sanders, Chesley and Charles Krohn, Tom Foral, Penny Metropulos, Richard Howard, John Corley, Thomas J. Lyttle, Mary Ruisard, Deirdre Spann, Claremarie Verheyen, Paul Rathburn, Liz Ayers, Linne Cain, and Anne Miner for patience in listening to my enthusiasm and for their encouragement. And to my editors, Suzanne Staszak-Silva and Karen Treat, my deep thanks for shepherding the book to publication.

Introduction

+⧎ ⧎+

We'll be friends first!

Much Ado About Nothing, act 4, scene 2

In *Richard II*, Shakespeare writes, "I count myself in nothing else so happy as a soul remembering my good friends." Despite the existence of many unknowns in William Shakespeare's life, it is possible to gain a glimpse into his personality by exploring the friendships of this man whose writings of three centuries ago are still required reading, whose plays still dominate today's theatre, and whose characters easily become friends to us all.

In *Shakespeare's Imagery*, Caroline Spurgeon observes:

There is one thought which we find recurring in his work in many forms. . . . To befriend, to support, to help, to cheer and illuminate our fellow-men is the whole object of our being, and if we fail to do this, we have failed in that object, and are as empty husks, hollow and meaningless.[1]

Examples of this valuing of friendship abound in Shakespeare's work, and the best and most satisfying of his plays show deep bonds of friendship between the leading characters.

In an early work, *The Taming of the Shrew*, Shakespeare explores the friendship between Petruchio and Hortensio as a minor plotline. Friendship subsequently becomes a recurrent motif, and often we observe that the development or betrayal of friendships defines a play's very structure. In *Two Gentlemen of Verona*, for instance, the story centers on the adventures of Proteus and Valentine, two young aristocrats whose friendship is tested by rivalry in love. More powerfully, in *The Merchant of Venice* Shakespeare shows Antonio risking his life to help his young friend Bassanio gain a wife. At the height of his powers, Shakespeare offers *Othello*, the tragedy of friendship betrayed, where the jealous Iago systematically destroys his former friend.

The friendships are not limited to a certain class or gender. *Richard II* depicts a king utterly dependent on his royal friends; *Henry IV, Parts 1* and *2* take Prince Hal to the Boar's Head Inn to carouse with his disreputable friends Falstaff, Peto, and Bardolph; *The Merry Wives of Windsor* lets us share in the friendship between two straight-laced, middle-class, middle-aged women. We see the theme expressed in words as well as action: in *Julius Caesar* the words "friend," "friends," or "friendship" occur thirty-two times; in *Two Gentlemen of Verona*, they appear thirty-seven times.

The word "friend" in English has the broadest possible connotation. It can refer to a relationship of profound intimacy or to one of barely more than acquaintance. It constantly requires modification: "She was my friend—not close, of course." "He was my oldest, dearest friend." "We were best friends in school." "Friends? Yes. Well, I *knew* her." While children in school try to determine who is their first best friend, their second best friend, or their third best friend, adults can read in a society column that this or that Hollywood star invited his five hundred closest friends to a birthday party. Rumors abounded in the mid–twentieth century regarding President John F. Kennedy's "friendship" with entertainer Frank Sinatra, and no one would have reacted with surprise to assertions that his wife was a "friend" to cellist Pablo Casals, or that Princess Margaret (a balletomane) was "friends" with Rudolf Nureyev or Margot Fonteyn. It is in this last context that I suggest William Shakespeare was friends with Queen Elizabeth I and King James I—a connection obviously far different from his deep intimacy with working colleagues Richard Burbage, John Heminges, and Henry Condell, or childhood friend Hamnet Sadler.

To be included in this book, the "friends" had to meet three criteria. First, there had to be evidence that Shakespeare knew each one, and that they knew him. Second, there had to be sufficient reason to believe the relationship Shakespeare had with them was cordial. And third, whether or not the relationship was intimate, an individual was included if the exploration of his or her relationship with Shakespeare could shed light on our knowledge of Shakespeare's daily life.

William Shakespeare was an extremely private individual. He fascinates us precisely because he left so little documentation about his life. But we know that one-third to one-half of the people represented here were very close to him: he left them bequests in his will, worked with them for over twenty years, or chose to live near them in his retirement. Other acquaintances remain elusive—the Countess of Pembroke, Lady Warwick, Michael Drayton, Philip Henslowe, and Edward Alleyn, for instance. He knew them, but no one can say how close he felt to them. Yet his relationship to each of them is revelatory and demonstrates to us the rich and varied social world in which he had a place.

The friendships represented in Shakespeare's plays include those between men and women, old and young, servant and master, king and fool. And like his characters, Shakespeare's own friendships cut across lines of class, age, religion, and gender. Some of his friends were actors and managers in the theatre. Some were writers like himself. Some were printers and publishers. Some were women, some children. A few were members of the aristocracy. More were classmates from his schooldays in Stratford—boyhood friends he kept his entire life.

As Shakespeare often made the friendships in his plays define the play structure, so his broad range of friendships help to define his life, each illuminating a different aspect of his character. The following, then, are Shakespeare's friends.

William Shakespeare
(1564–1616)

When and Where Shakespeare Met the Friends Whose
Lives Are Detailed in This Book

> Warwickshire lad, all be glad,
> For the lad of all lads was a Warwickshire lad.
>
> *The Warwickshire Lad*, Charles Dibdin
> (eighteenth-century song)

William Shakespeare's name first appears on April 26, 1564, in the records of the Church of the Holy Trinity, Stratford-upon-Avon. Written in Latin, it registers his baptism. His parents were John Shakespeare, a glover and wool dealer residing on Henley Street, and Mary, his wife, the eighth daughter of a wealthy landowning farmer from nearby Wilmcote. Mary and John's first two children, both girls, died in infancy, and the year 1564 was a perilous time in which to have another child: the plague was ravaging England and had settled with deadly effect on Stratford just at the time of Shakespeare's birth.

Shakespeare survived, however, and grew up in a distinguished household. His father was a member of the Corporation, Stratford's governing body, holding the offices of ale-taster, then councilman, constable, chamberlain, alderman, and finally bailiff—the equivalent of mayor. With this last honor came the right to have a reserved pew in the church and, among other responsibilities, to grant licenses to the increasing number of traveling theatre companies, which first began coming to Stratford in 1569, five years after Shakespeare's birth.

In addition to William, the Shakespeares' family of young children grew to include Gilbert, Joan, Anne, Richard, and Edmund. Eight-year-old Anne died in 1579 when her older brother William was fifteen, one year before the last child, Edmund, was born.

Boys in Elizabethan England, and often girls, learned to read and write at home, or they were schooled by the parish clerk or a "petty school" (the equivalent of our preschool). At about age seven, the boys in Stratford were able to enter King Edward VI's free school, informally called the Stratford grammar school. Assuming he followed the normal pattern, William Shakespeare joined his friends **Richard Quiney**, **Hamnet Sadler**, **Richard Tyler**, and **Richard Field**, attending classes there until he was about fifteen.

In 1576, John Shakespeare's speculation in wool-dealing sent his fortunes into a long decline. He was absent from council meetings and ceased going to church for fear of being dunned for unpaid debts. As the months and years dragged on, he mortgaged, then lost, the property that had come as part of his wife's dowry.

In the midst of this family misfortune, their oldest son brought more trouble home. On November 27, 1582, in the village of Temple Grafton, five miles west of Stratford, a marriage license was issued to "Willilmom Shaxpere et Annam Whateley de Temple Grafton." The next day, Fulk Sandells and John Richardson, Stratford friends of the bride, entered into a bond with the Bishop of Worcester for forty pounds. The bond said that "William Shagspere" was to marry Anne Hathaway of Stratford, and that the Bishop would be held harmless against any impediments which might later be announced against the marriage. The normal three-week announcement of banns could not be scheduled since Advent, a penitential season during which marriages could not take place, was fast approaching. A special license for an immediate marriage was necessary as Anne Hathaway was pregnant. Sandells and Richardson had to act for Shakespeare because he was still a minor.

Several questions arise: Why did his father not act for Shakespeare? And who was Anne Whateley? Anne Hathaway was from Shottery and Stratford; if she was the "Anne" in question, why were she and Shakespeare married in Temple Grafton? Romantics create a story of two Annes; they say that Shakespeare planned to marry Anne Whateley, whom he loved, but was prevented by the hasty intervention of the pregnant Anne Hathaway, whose friends forced him to marry her instead. The less dramatic theory points to a distracted clerk who was registering a dispute concerning a William Whateley at the same time, and who simply wrote down the wrong name.

In any event, Shakespeare married Anne Hathaway, and their daughter Susanna was born six months later. Twins, named for Shakespeare's friends **Judith** and **Hamnet Sadler**, followed two years later. Shakespeare was a husband and the father of three children before the age of twenty-one. As he had no separate address in Stratford, he apparently lived with his wife, three children, four siblings, and his parents in the family house on Henley Street.

Shakespeare's activity in Stratford during this period is undocumented. Some scholars find the tradition and evidence that he was a school-master most convincing; others, analyzing the skill and instinct with which he uses legal terminology in his plays, suggest he worked with one or another of Stratford's lawyers; perhaps, like some of his friends, he worked in his father's trade.

What is known is that in 1587, two years after the twins' birth, five different theatre companies performed in Stratford. One of them, the Earl of Leicester's company, had long-time connections in Warwickshire. At the company's head was James Burbage, father of **Richard Burbage**, with whom Shakespeare would soon be working in London. Another company, the Queen's Company, had recently lost one of its actors.

Perhaps it is no coincidence that the next document concerning William Shakespeare connects the young Stratfordian with the London theatre. In 1592, in a pamphlet called *Greene's Groats-worth of Witte, bought with a million of Repentance*, playwright and pamphleteer Robert Greene warned his fellow scholars that:

> there is an upstart crow, beautified with our feathers, that with his "Tyger's heart wrapped in a player's hide" supposes he is as well able to bombast out a blank verse as the best of you: and being an absolute "Johannes factotum" is in his own conceit the only Shakescene in a country.[1]

The "tiger's heart wrapped in a player's hide" mocks Shakespeare's description of Queen Margaret in *Henry VI, Part 3*: "Oh tiger's heart wrapp'd in a woman's hide!" So between the baptism of Shakespeare's twins in 1585 and the appearance of Greene's pamphlet in 1592, Shakespeare moved to London, became a working actor, and wrote his first historical plays, the three-part *Henry VI*. He also became acquainted with many of the great men of the Elizabethan theatre: playwright **Christopher Marlowe**; actor **Edward Alleyn**; manager **Philip Henslowe**; the Burbage family, who had built London's first free-standing playhouse, the Theatre; and patrons like the **Earl of Pembroke**.

From 1592 to 1594, an outbreak of the plague closed the theatres in London. Acting companies were forced to take to the road. Shakespeare used this time to write his two epic poems—*Venus and Adonis* and *The Rape of Lucrece*—dedicating both of them to a young and glamorous aristocrat, Henry Wriothesley, the **Earl of Southampton**. Internal evidence suggests that Shakespeare's *Sonnets* were written during this time, and that Southampton was the young man to whom they were addressed.

In 1594 the plague ended. Actors returned to London, reorganizing themselves under different managements and patrons. Henry Carey, Lord Hunsdon, became patron of the group of actors known, because of his title, as the Lord Chamberlain's Men. In addition to Shakespeare, this company included **Thomas Pope**, **Augustine Phillips**, George Bryan, and **John Heminges**; **Will Kempe**, the famous comedian; and Richard Burbage, the actor for whom Shakespeare would write his greatest leading roles.

Shakespeare bought shares in the company, perhaps with the money paid to him by Southampton for his poems. He was the only playwright of his era to hold ownership in the company for which he wrote, and the only one to write exclusively for a single company. His fortune, though, was not based on payment for his plays, but on his acting and his shareholding in the company.

In those early years, he became the company's major playwright. Close to the time of *Henry VI, Parts 1, 2,* and *3,* he wrote *Richard III, Titus Andronicus, The Taming of the Shrew, Comedy of Errors, Two Gentlemen of Verona,* and *Love's Labours Lost.* In *Love's Labours Lost* Shakespeare unleashed his great lyric gift, which distinguishes the plays that follow: *A Midsummer Night's Dream, Romeo and Juliet,* and *Richard II.*

While other actors in the company—John Heminges and Thomas Pope, for instance, or the Burbages—were married and owned houses in London (which they filled with children, servants, and acting apprentices), Shakespeare lived quietly in a sequence of rented lodgings. His name first appears on the tax roles of St. Helen's parish, an aristocratic neighborhood on Bishopsgates Street. This street becomes Shoreditch Road to the north, outside the city walls. Here, near rural Finsbury Fields, rose the Theatre and the Curtain where Shakespeare's early plays were produced.

Later, Shakespeare moved south, across the Thames River, to Southwark in the Liberty of the Clink. A lawsuit hounded him there for back taxes claimed by St. Helen's Parish. The suit wound up in the hands of the Bishop of Winchester, in whose jurisdiction the parish lay, and where it seems the taxes were eventually paid.

There, outside London and free from many of its restrictions, theatres existed side by side with bearbaiting arenas, prisons, brothels, inns, residences, taverns, churches, and the palace of the Bishop. Back and forth across the river, ferrymen brought Londoners to Southwark for their entertainment, and in this lively spot the Chamberlain's Men built the Globe Theatre in 1598. (For details, see the entry on **Cuthbert Burbage**.)

By this time, Shakespeare had written the works of his middle years: *King John*, *The Merchant of Venice*, *Henry IV*, *Parts 1* and *2*, and *The Merry Wives of Windsor*. The claim arose early in the eighteenth century (according to the gossipy John Dennis in 1702) that this last play was specifically requested by **Queen Elizabeth I**—who wanted to see Falstaff in love—and that Shakespeare complied by writing the script in just two weeks.[2] Whatever the truth of the story, the Queen admired the Chamberlain's Men and brought them to court for performances more than any of the other London companies. By the end of the 1590s, Shakespeare was distinguished enough to receive the coat of arms his father had long desired for the family, and wealthy enough to buy, in 1597, the second largest house in Stratford: New Place.

"Will fortune never come with both hands full?" King Henry IV cries out in the second of the plays that bear his name. Indeed, Shakespeare's satisfaction in his success and wealth were undermined by the death, in 1596, of his only son, eleven-year-old Hamnet. We can hear the echo of Shakespeare's own sorrow in the lines of Constance grieving over her son in *King John*:

> Grief fills the room up of my absent child:
> Lies in his bed, walks up and down with me,
> Puts on his pretty looks, repeats his words,
> Remembers me of all his gracious parts,
> Stuffs out his vacant garments with his form;
> Then have I reason to be fond of grief....
> O Lord! My boy, my Arthur, my fair son!
> My life, my joy, my food, my all the world!
> My widow-comfort, and my sorrow's cure.

> *King John*, act 3, scene 4

A new, darker thread weaves through the vibrant fabric of the plays that follow: *Much Ado About Nothing, Henry V, Julius Caesar, As You Like It, Twelfth Night*. These are the first great plays of Shakespeare's maturity. Each is enriched by characters who explore moments of deep melancholy and aloneness.

In 1601 politics in London took a dramatic turn when the Earl of Essex, Queen Elizabeth's favorite and, like Hamlet, "the glass of fashion and the mold of form," led an ill-fated rebellion against the aging queen. He paid for it with his life. Shakespeare's patron, the Earl of Southampton, a follower of the dashing Essex, was jailed in the Tower. The Lord Chamberlain's Men were brought to court to defend their production of *Richard II*, performed at the request of the followers of Essex just before the rebellion. This was the nearest Shakespeare and his friends came to punishment for their work. That they were excused is an example of the respect in which the queen held their company.

The same year, 1601, Shakespeare's father died. The following year his friend Richard Quiney died. And in 1603 Queen Elizabeth, who had ruled England since before Shakespeare's birth, reached the end of her extraordinary life.

During the years 1600 to 1603, Shakespeare wrote two of his great tragedies, *Hamlet* and *Othello*, as well as the complex and experimental comedy-dramas *Troilus and Cressida* and *All's Well That Ends Well*. At the same time, he bought more property in Stratford. In May 1602, he purchased 127 acres from **John** and **William Combe**, and a few months later he bought the lease on a cottage in Chapel Lane across from New Place.

Shakespeare, ever on the move, took up residence in about 1602 with Christopher and **Maria Mountjoy** in Silver Street, Cripplegate. This location placed him back north of the Thames in St. Olave's parish, near his friends **Henry Condell** and John Heminges. The last record of Shakespeare's performing as an actor was 1603; so this move, which placed him farther from the Globe, was less inconvenient than it would have been in earlier years. Here he was not far from the Mermaid Tavern, where some of his colleagues enjoyed congregating, and where he struck up a friendship with the owner, **William Johnson**.

In 1603, when **James I** became king, he honored Shakespeare and his company by granting them royal patronage. From now on, they would be known as the King's Men. Shakespeare continued to explore the tragic vein with *King Lear* and *Macbeth*, and the dark comic genre with *Measure for Measure*. Between 1604 and 1608, *Antony and*

Cleopatra, *Timon of Athens*, and *Coriolanus*—inspired by the release of a new edition of North's *Lives of the Ancient Greeks and Romans*—mark Shakespeare's return to the classical subject matter he had earlier mined when writing *Titus Andronicus*, *Julius Caesar*, and *Troilus and Cressida*.

In 1607 Shakespeare's youngest brother, Edmund, died at age twenty-seven. At some point Edmund had followed Shakespeare to London, where he, too, became a player. Edmund fathered an illegitimate son named Edward who died and was buried at St. Gile's Cripplegate, just four months before the death of his father. Edmund was buried at St. Savior's Southwark on December 31, 1607. The sexton notes the "forenoon knell of the great bell, xx shillings," indicating a costly morning funeral, probably paid for by Shakespeare, and arranged so that the actors, attending this sad memorial for a young colleague—the brother of a friend—would be able to play their afternoon performance. Then, as now, the show must go on.

In addition to the Globe Theatre, the Burbages owned an indoor theatre, the Blackfriars. In 1608 the King's Men took over the lease, created a new investment group of "householders" (which included Shakespeare), and began performing their plays in this indoor space. Shakespeare's late romances—*Cymbeline*, *The Winter's Tale*, and *The Tempest* (1609–1611)—move into a realm of fantasy, reflecting the production capabilities of the new indoor space and the tastes of a more select audience.

In 1611 Shakespeare came home to live in Stratford, retiring from his full-time activities in the theatre, and taking up the life of a landowning countryman. It was not easy to leave London completely. In 1612 he was called back to be a witness in a suit brought by Stephen Belott, a former apprentice of the Mountjoys, who had married the Mountjoys' daughter and who was claiming not to have received his promised dowry. In his deposition Shakespeare acknowledged his help in the courtship of the couple, but claimed to have no recollection of what was promised in the marriage settlement. At about the same time he wrote *Henry VIII*, the last play attributed to him with certainty.

In March of 1613 Shakespeare came to London again. This time he bought his only London property, the Blackfriars Gatehouse, a residential property he subsequently leased out. Further, he helped his good friend Richard Burbage design an "impresa," or symbolic shield, for Lord Rutland to carry in the tenth-year celebration of the accession of James I.

At Christmas of 1614 the Stratford Corporation Accounts lists payment of twenty-two pence for "one quart of sack and one quart of claret wine given to a preacher at the New Place." It would seem, then, that Shakespeare hosted a public event at his home, but this is the only evidence we have of his hospitality, or of any connection with public life in Stratford.

Shakespeare was still listed as a shareholder in the Globe and Blackfriars companies in the *Ostler v. Heminges* lawsuit in 1615, but no more evidence takes him to London. During his five years of retirement in Stratford, he at last had time with his family, though no one will ever know the quality of his relationship with his wife Anne. Other relatives include Dr. **John Hall**, his son-in-law, who was a distinguished colleague only thirteen years his junior; his daughter Susanna, a woman (according to her tombstone) "witty above her sex"; and his granddaughter Elizabeth, who was at that time progressing through the entrancing years of three to eight. His second daughter, Judith, undoubtedly provided drama and spice as she was approaching her thirties, unmarried, and attracted to the black sheep of the Quiney family.

Shakespeare kept up friendly relations with the Combes, the **Nash family**, the Quineys, **William Reynolds**, **Thomas Greene** and his family, **Thomas Russell**, **Alexander Aspinall**, and **Julius Shaw**.

In January of 1616 he arranged with his lawyer and friend, **Francis Collins**, to make the first draft of his will. In February his daughter Judith married Thomas, the third son of his old friend Richard Quiney. The young man was a ne'er-do-well and Shakespeare was worried about the marriage, so he revised the will in March, altering his provisions for Judith as well as making other amendments.

One of the persistent legends about Shakespeare, originated by the Stratford vicar John Ward more than half a century after Shakespeare's death, is that his literary friends **Ben Jonson** and **Michael Drayton** came to visit him and took him out for a "merry meeting" after which, having drunk too much, Shakespeare caught a fever and died. The legend lives, though it has no factual basis, because we want to believe that at the end of his life, Shakespeare's good friends came to see him, and that before dying he had at least one more merry meeting.

Shakespeare died on April 23, 1616, and is buried in the Church of the Holy Trinity, Stratford, where he had been baptized fifty-two years before.

Shakespeare's Stratford Friends

＋＝ ＝＋

In Which We See What Life Was Like for Shakespeare and
His Friends in Sixteenth-Century Stratford-upon-Avon

Tell me what company you keep, and I'll tell you what you are.
Don Quixote, Miguel de Cervantes (1547–1616)

In Shakespeare's day, a thousand elm trees shaded the unpaved roads
of Stratford.[1] William Shakespeare and his friends Hamnet Sadler,
Richard Field, Richard Tyler, and Richard Quiney lived and played in
half-timbered houses that faced the street and that hid gardens and
orchards in back. Farmland and woodland, including the Forest of
Arden, surrounded the town, while the gentle Avon River, with swans
drifting on the current, flowed as it does today under the Clopton
Bridge.

This arched stone structure felt the clop of many a horse's hoof and
the rattle and creaking of many a carriage. The boys could watch as the
world came from London through Stratford to the great houses of
Warwickshire: Warwick Castle to the north; Kenilworth Castle (the
home of Queen Elizabeth's favorite, the Earl of Leicester) a bit nearer;
and, just four miles to the east, Charlecote, home of Sir Thomas Lucy.
Here the teenaged William Shakespeare was said to have poached a
deer, and here Queen Elizabeth came to stay in 1566 and 1572.

Every Thursday, farmers brought their produce and stock to the market square in Stratford where they bartered or purchased what they needed from the town craftsmen and artisans. These included weavers, saddlers, ale and beer makers, smiths, carpenters, bakers, butchers, hatters and haberdashers, mercers, and glovers.

Shakespeare's father would set up with the glovers' stalls, pitched by the building called High Cross. Nearby was the whipping post where, as they helped their fathers sell their goods, Shakespeare and Sadler and the three Richards would have from time to time seen local miscreants—vagabonds, loose women, thieves—publicly flogged.

Estimates for Stratford's population in the late sixteenth century range from about 1,200 to about 2,000; whichever figure is accurate, the number doubled on market days, and Stratford was considered one of the most important towns in Warwickshire.

For recreation Will and his friends ran, jumped, and played leapfrog or hide-and-seek. Or they could learn from their parents, who, when not hard at work, fished in the river, swam, played at bowls, developed their skills with the bow and arrow, set traps for birds or other small animals, or met at the inns or taverns—women as well as men—to drink and visit. Local musicians played in a town band; the whole community produced a religious festival in the spring at Whitsuntide; and, beginning in 1569, professional theatre companies began stopping in Stratford to perform.

Weekdays were working days for young and old alike. Before daylight Shakespeare and the other children in Stratford's roughly 240 households were roused and made to wash, then to clean their teeth with a cloth and sweet paste. They dressed and heard morning prayers, kneeling for their parents' blessing. After a breakfast of bread, butter, and cheese, the boys hurried off carrying satchels containing hornbooks, ink, quills, and knives for trimming the quills into pens.

King Edward's New School, a free school open to all sons of Stratford burgesses, consisted of a single room on the second floor of the Guild Hall, three streets over from the house where Shakespeare was born. About forty boys ages seven to fifteen gathered in the 6 A.M. darkness for devotions and singing from the Psalter in the Guild Chapel. They then clambered up the stairs to take their places on hard, unpadded benches behind scarred wooden desks. However tempted by the distraction offered by windows looking out over Church Street, they were made to work from early morning to late afternoon.

Sundays also demanded effort from the boys as they had to attend church services and listen closely to the vicar in order to report on his sermon at school the next day. The Stratford vicar from 1569 to 1584 was Henry Heicroft, a fellow of St. John's Cambridge, and the holder of an M.A. degree. His preaching was part of the education of Stratford's children, and only after analyzing Sunday's lesson did the boys turn from Master Heicroft's sermon to their Lily and Colet's *Latin Grammar*.

Shakespeare's intellectual friend, the playwright Ben Jonson, tells us that Shakespeare had "small Latin and less Greek,"[2] but his remark must be understood in relation to the schooling of the time. In Shakespeare's day, the "trivium,"—the study of Latin grammar, logic, and rhetoric, including literature and history—was the dominant element of the first four years of every boy's education. The preeminence of Latin language study gave "grammar schools" the name they go by to this day. The "quadrivium" followed, which added arithmetic, geometry, astronomy, and music to the curriculum; but little boys spent most of their time, from seven in the morning until six in the evening, reading, memorizing, conjugating, declining, analyzing, reciting, and writing Latin. In the process, they learned over two hundred Latin rhetorical patterns by name, which they had to define; they then had to be able to recognize them in writings from Cicero to Caesar to Virgil, and use them in Latin compositions of their own. In addition, they translated from Latin to English, and English to Latin, passages from the Geneva Bible.

Quotations from Proverbs, Psalms, Genesis, Job, both Ecclesiastes, and the apocryphal book Ecclesiasticus abound in Shakespeare's plays. They were fixed in his mind as a child. And the extraordinary rhetorical skills he demonstrated—although enlivened with his poetic imagination and unmatched dramatic instincts—had been inculcated in him through rigorous training in the Stratford Grammar School.

A good memory was prized and rewarded in this environment, as each morning's lesson had to be repeated the next day "without book," and on Friday the whole week's work had to be known by heart perfectly. When twenty-first-century actors marvel that an Elizabethan acting company could perform anywhere from fifteen to forty plays in a single season, it must be remarked that the prodigious capacity to memorize and retain words was taught from a very young age.

Moreover, actor training of a kind took place in the school curriculum. The comedies of Terence and Plautus were learned by heart for performance, and the boys were encouraged to recite with feeling. Canons from the bishop demanded that they stand up straight and speak loudly and distinctly. Richard Field, Hamnet Sadler, and

William Shakespeare learned together, from books like Cullmann's *Sententias Pueriles*, Latin proverbs and sayings to be used in conversations which they practiced with one another. Over two hundred references to *Sententias Pueriles* have been found in Shakespeare's plays, the most recognizable undoubtedly being the precepts Polonius gives his son Laertes in *Hamlet*.

From 1571 to 1575 the master of the upper school was Simon Hunt, who held a B.A. from Oxford. Paid a generous salary of twenty pounds, Hunt shared this fee with his assistant, called the usher, who taught the younger boys.

In 1575 Thomas Jenkins, who had earned his M.A. at Oxford, replaced Simon Hunt. Jenkins introduced the boys to Quintilian and Ovid, Virgil and Horace, and the Greek New Testament, among many other now long-neglected classical works. Says Chiron in *Titus Andronicus* (4.2), one of Shakespeare's early plays:

> Oh, 'tis a verse from Horace; I know it well.
> I read it in the grammar long ago.

Schooled in formal argument, the students constructed forceful emotional debates in which they were made to argue both sides with equal fervor. One imagines that the future author of the funeral scene in *Julius Caesar*, who gives such eloquent voice to both Brutus and Mark Antony, showed some gift at this exercise.

The carry-over from his schooldays is apparent elsewhere. Many quotations from Shakespeare's schoolbooks appear in his plays; the rhythms, stories, and symbols from the Bible resound through his work; and characters like Holofernes in *Love's Labours Lost* and Sir Hugh Evans in *The Merry Wives of Windsor* show that the memory of his schooling remained fresh in the adult Shakespeare's mind.

Occasionally the children would be given a break from their hard work and would celebrate with a "barring out" day. They would shut the door against the master and give way to a rowdiness that at least once, in the time of Mr. Hunt, required payment for a broken window.

Under the tutelage of a series of these fine, well-qualified teachers, a number of young men progressed from Stratford Grammar School directly to Oxford or Cambridge. Shakespeare did not. Why? Perhaps his father's financial reversals kept the family from sending the oldest son away. Maybe Shakespeare's gifts were creative rather than intellectual. Or his early marriage might have interrupted plans for university study. Whatever the reason, it was not inadequate grammar school instruction.

Shakespeare forged his early, lasting friendships while struggling through his lessons in the second-floor classroom and the courtyard of the Stratford Grammar School. As boys of all ages were taught together, the youngest, Richard Tyler, along with Will Shakespeare, Hamnet Sadler, and Richard Field witnessed the higher education of Richard Quiney, a neighbor boy and friend six or seven years their senior.

Richard Quiney (c. 1557–1602)

Then the whining school-boy, with his satchel
And shining morning face, creeping like snail
Unwillingly to school.

As You Like It, act 2, scene 7

The Quineys and the Shakespeares lived near each other and Richard's and William's grandfathers—old Richard Quiney and Richard Shakespeare of Snitterfield—knew each other. Their fathers, Adrian Quiney and John Shakespeare, were neighbors for over fifty years and served together on the Stratford town council where each had risen to be bailiff. William Shakespeare's friend Richard Quiney was born in the late 1550s. His father was a wealthy mercer (dealer in dry goods, textiles, and groceries) and a gentleman continuously active in town politics.

A letter still exists from Quiney to his father, in Latin with careful handwriting, written when Quiney was eleven years old. And his school Latin stayed with him: Edgar Fripp, in *Master Richard Quyny*, tells us that as an adult, Quiney took Tully's *Epistles*, in Latin, with him on a trip for reading matter.

After leaving school Quiney became a partner in his father's business, according to Fripp selling "green taffeta, fustian, skeins of silk, silk buttons, Southwich cloth, Worcestershire hose" (p. 45), as well as metal for bells, red lead, tiles, and bricks. The Quineys also dealt in farm products and malt.

On January 24, 1580, Richard Quiney married Elizabeth Phillips. On September 7 that same year, he was elected a principal burgess. His father was so proud of him that he made note of it in the Corporation records (as the Stratford town's governing organization was called), and made a gift to the Corporation in honor of the occasion: upon his death the city would receive one mark of the rent due him from a property he owned on Church Street.

In 1582, the year of Shakespeare's marriage, Elizabeth, the first of the Quineys' nine children, was born. By 1588 Richard Quiney was an alderman on the town council. His subsequent years of service give us much information via the surviving letters he wrote to his friend Abraham Sturley, and the many Borough records in his handwriting. Even as a young man, he was a distinguished citizen and public servant.

In contrast, in about 1588 William Shakespeare left his family in Stratford. He walked away from steady, traditional employment and any form of public service. He set off for London, pursuing his ambition to become an actor in the heady, unpredictable, disreputable world of the theatre.

Richard Quiney and William Shakespeare: The Later Connection

In the Stratford Records Office, a blue leather cover and plastic shield protects a yellowing piece of paper covered on one side with small faded brown words. This is the only letter to the Stratford playwright that has survived the years. It is from Richard Quiney, and he addresses Shakespeare as "Loveinge good ffrend & countreyman Mr Wm Shackespere."

Once he became an alderman and bailiff, Richard Quiney often traveled on Stratford town business. London was a common destination: he went there every year from 1597 to 1601. In 1598 he came seeking loans for Stratford, which had twice been devastated by fires (in 1594 and 1595). He was also applying to the national government for a new corporation charter and relief for the beleaguered town from taxation recently voted by Parliament.

Quiney was kept waiting four months as he tried to negotiate for the city. He needed thirty pounds to pay off urgent debts which he had incurred in this service. William Shakespeare's success had become obvious to his Stratford friends and family the year before when he bought New Place, the second-largest home in Stratford. As the price of the house was sixty pounds, the amount of Quiney's requested loan is impressive. But Quiney's old acquaintance and neighbor, Abraham Sturley, had written to Richard Quiney in January 1598 that William Shakespeare was "willing to disburse some money"[3] on the possible purchase of lands near Shottery; so it seemed to Sturley and Quiney that their townsfellow, the actor William Shakespeare, might have an additional thirty pounds to lend. Richard Quiney wrote his letter from a London inn on Bell and Carter Lane near St. Paul's, and dated it October 25, 1598. He follows the salutation "Loving Countryman" with "I am bold of you as of a friend."[4]

For Shakespeare, the request for a loan must have brought with it a sense of poetic justice. Richard Quiney had followed the pattern of his own father's life—the life Shakespeare's father must have wished and envisioned for his son. What affirmation of Shakespeare's choice to leave Stratford to follow a theatrical career could be sweeter than that, ten years later, the Bailiff of Stratford, Richard Quiney, should come to him in need of money?

The text of the "Loving Countryman" letter immediately focuses on a shared love of home and childhood as the basis for the request. But the letter seems not to have been delivered; it languished in the Quiney file of the Stratford archives until it was discovered in 1793. We do not know if Quiney visited Shakespeare in person, or if Shakespeare ever made such a loan. However, Abraham Sturley, who first suggested the request be made to Shakespeare, wrote six days later on November 4 that "our countryman Mr. Wm. Shak. would procure us money . . . which I shall like of as I shall hear when, where and how."[5] So it seems Shakespeare was willing. The need for the loan was obviated, though, when Queen Elizabeth granted the tax relief to Stratford ("this town twice afflicted and almost wasted by fire"[6]), and Quiney's expenses were reimbursed by the exchequer.

Shakespeare took little or no interest in the government of Stratford. He retired there; he had made canny investments in real estate and tithes; but, unlike his father and the Quineys, he participated little in the public life of his hometown. Richard Quiney's passionate involvement, in contrast, brought him once again to William Shakespeare's London, this time in some disgrace.

In 1601 Quiney quarreled with Sir Edward Greville, the local squire, when Greville tried to enclose the Stratford town common. In response Quiney and others gathered to tear down the enclosing hedges. They were arrested for rioting. The leaders were remanded to Marshalsea Prison in Southwark, London, for encouraging the uprising. Shakespeare was living in Southwark at that time and the irony that becomes a leitmotif in this relationship reappears: Quiney, the respectable man from Stratford comes to London to be imprisoned for rioting, while Shakespeare, the follower of a disreputable trade has become rich, settled, and conservative. But Quiney was not in prison long; he raised bail and soon returned to Stratford.

The Grevilles' next suit against Richard Quiney claimed that they, not the town, had the right to appoint toll-gatherers for the Stratford fair. Quiney filed a countersuit and, later in 1601, traveled to London again, this time with Shakespeare's "cousin" Thomas Greene (then solicitor of Stratford), to seek advice from the Crown's attorney general on the matter. In May of 1602, a drunken band of Greville's men, whom Quiney as bailiff was trying to calm down, wounded Quiney, and he died from the assault.

John Shakespeare had died the year before. We can imagine the effect of Richard Quiney's death on Shakespeare, just eight months after losing his father. *Hamlet* was registered with the stationer in July of 1602, so in the background of that great play—the story of a complicated father–son relationship filled with the deaths of relatives and friends—the loss of his father and his old friend must have filled the consciousness of Shakespeare the writer, and Shakespeare the man.

The friendships of the Shakespeare and the Quiney families did not end with the death of Richard. While Shakespeare worked in London, his wife Anne lived in Stratford near Quiney's widow, Elizabeth ("Bess"), who upon Richard's death was left with their nine children all under twenty years of age. She supported them by keeping a tavern, and one of them, the black sheep Thomas, married Shakespeare's daughter Judith. Another Quiney son, George, a Balliol graduate ("of good wit and expert in languages," according to Dr. Hall[7]), returned to Stratford to become curate at the church and assistant at the school. Dr. Hall, who was married to Shakespeare's daughter Susanna, treated George for tuberculosis, but George died of the disease at age twenty-four.

The name Quiney is familiar in Stratford to this day, preserved by the descendents of the family. Shakespeare's name permeates the town only because of his work. Marchette Chute, in *Shakespeare of London*, emphasizes how Shakespeare's will reveals his care to amass an inheritance to be left to his descendents. "As Shakespeare's will shows, he was determined to leave all his property intact to a single male heir, and he did not want the land he had protected so carefully to be dissolved into alien hands" (p. 307). Shakespeare did not value the heritage of his work. In spite of the repeated claims in the sonnets that his lines would outlast time, Shakespeare took no care, in his maturity, to publish or preserve his writing. We can surmise that Shakespeare would have burned every one of his plays and poems, if doing so could have saved the life of his son Hamnet, and allowed him, like Richard Quiney, to leave his fortune to descendents of his name. But after Hamnet's death at age eleven, Shakespeare had only daughters left. Judith Shakespeare Quiney's children—the last named Shakespeare Quiney—died young, while Susannah Shakespeare Hall's daughter Elizabeth died childless. The care William Shakespeare took to preserve his estate for his heirs was to no avail.

The irony William Shakespeare expressed so often in his plays was lived out in his own life. The great writer, who wanted to father a line of descendents to whom he could leave the land, the coat of arms, and the fortune he had worked so hard to acquire, like one of the left-out characters at the end of his great comedies, died with no sons to carry on his name. Meanwhile, Richard Quiney, remembered for writing just one ordinary letter addressing William Shakespeare as his "Loving Countryman," has descendents in Warwickshire to this day.

Hamnet Sadler (c. 1562–1624)

Home keeping youth have ever homely wits...
I rather would entreat thy company
To see the wonders of the world abroad
Than, living dully sluggardized at home
Wear out thy youth with shapeless idleness.
                Two Gentlemen of Verona, act 1, scene 1

Hamnet Sadler was born in about 1562 into a family that had lived in Stratford since the fourteenth century. Closer in age to Shakespeare than Richard Quiney, Sadler must have often been Shakespeare's companion, hurrying to school or playing in the fields on their rare days off.

In the late 1570s, close to the time he inherited his father Roger Sadler's bakery along with a house on High Street, young Hamnet Sadler married Judith (probably Judith Staunton of Longbridge). Hamnet and Judith Sadler had fourteen children, seven of whom died in infancy. During their marriage, which lasted over three decades, the Sadlers lived at the corner of High Street and Sheep Street, just two blocks from the Shakespeares' house on Henley Street.

In 1582 eighteen-year-old William Shakespeare married Anne Hathaway. His wife was older than he and pregnant. If the marriage were not completely of his choice, perhaps William Shakespeare found it a comfort and to have Hamnet Sadler, who also married early and had children, living nearby. In any event, confirming their deep friendship, William and Anne Shakespeare named the twins born to them in 1585 Hamnet and Judith, and the Sadlers were in all likelihood the godparents.

However similar their childhoods and youth, the pattern of Hamnet Sadler's adult life was the reverse of his friend Shakespeare's.

The Shakespeares and the Sadlers in Later Years

Shakespeare moved to London where, once established, his career went from triumph to triumph, gaining for him great wealth, a coat of arms, and the ownership of a the second-finest house in Stratford. Hamnet Sadler's life, meanwhile, became more and more difficult. On September 21, 1595, Sadler, with many mouths to feed, saw his bakery burn to the ground in one of the disastrous fires that swept through Stratford that decade.

In 1597, having bought the right to help collect money for fire relief, Sadler traveled on this business with Richard Quiney to Suffolk, Norfolk, and London. Any monies Sadler gained personally in this endeavor failed to help him for long, however, as he was repeatedly sued by creditors in the years that followed.

In 1598 (the same year Richard Quiney wrote to borrow money from his well-to-do "loving countryman," Shakespeare) the Sadlers had a son they named William. Shakespeare's purchase of New Place the previous year confirmed his intention to make Stratford his home. Perhaps the naming and baptism of William Sadler was a welcome back to Stratford for Shakespeare, and an insistent reminder from the Sadlers of their long friendship.

In May of 1606 the Sadlers, Susanna Shakespeare Hall (Shakespeare's eldest daughter), and eighteen other Stratford citizens were charged in the local ecclesiastical court with not having received Holy Communion on Easter Sunday. This observance was mandated by King James following the Gunpowder Plot, a failed Catholic attempt to destroy the government. The case against the Stratford group was dismissed, but it reminds us of the difficult question of religion in Shakespeare's time, when observances were dictated by changing governments.

Until the reign of Henry VIII, the religion of the sovereign, the people, the state, and the Roman Catholic Church were one and the same. Henry VIII's objection to the pope's refusal to grant him a divorce separated the English church from Roman Catholic papal domination; the King declared it illegal for his subjects to remain Catholic. For the first time English citizens were conflicted in their loyalties to their king and their religion.

Henry's son Edward VI was controlled by the Protestant advisers of his father. But his reign was a brief six years, and when at his early death his half-sister Mary became queen, loyalty to her Catholic mother (whom Henry had divorced) and to her own beliefs compelled her to declare it illegal for English people to remain Protestant. The very actions they had been required as loyal citizens to perform, overnight became actions that could send them to be burned at the stake. Mary ruled for only five years, however. Her successor, Elizabeth I, changed the rules again, returning the country to a compulsory Protestantism.

As a result of these changes, it was difficult for an individual citizen to define himself as Protestant or Catholic. In outward performance the family of John Shakespeare (who was born Catholic and lived through all the changes from Henry and Edward to Mary to Elizabeth) adhered to the state church of the day. But a document (cited in the eighteenth century and since lost) was found hidden in the walls of the Shakespeare house, indicating that John Shakespeare was a secret Catholic. Other historians note his compliance, while on the Stratford council, in hiring conservative clergymen and in painting over the Catholic murals in the Guild Hall Chapel, and conclude he was a devout Protestant.

But there were many secret Catholics in the Stratford area. Robert Catesby, whose recusant family owned the manor of Bishopton in Stratford and other property (Lapworth) north of town, supported his cousin who originated the Gunpowder Plot. Clopton House in Stratford was a meeting place for the conspirators, as was London's Mermaid Tavern, which Shakespeare frequented. Shakespeare knew of these men.

Anyone who exhibited Catholic sympathies at that time was suspected and feared. Hamnet and Judith Sadler and Susanna Shakespeare, when cited for missing the Easter Sacrament, had to promise to "cleanse their consciousness" and receive communion the next day. This exonerated them, and they had no further scrapes with the established church.

William Shakespeare conformed to expected religious observances; doing so never seemed to have been a problem for him. Was he Protestant like his possibly puritanical wife, or Catholic like his mother's family and, possibly, his father? We don't know. He kept his religious beliefs as private as his politics.

Though the Sadlers had no more religious trouble, their financial difficulties continued. In 1611, the year Shakespeare moved into his lavish New Place, the Sadlers' home was reported as being out of repair. Three years later, Judith Sadler died and Hamnet, alone after some thirty-four years of marriage, sold the lease of his house.

In 1616 a curious entry in Shakespeare's will makes us speculate on this long friendship. Hamnet Sadler was one of the witnesses, and is mentioned in the will, revised the month before Shakespeare died. But, as a beneficiary of twenty-six shillings and eight pence for the purchase of a ring, Sadler's name replaces that of Richard Tyler, Sadler and Shakespeare's schoolboy friend. In 1614 Richard Tyler had been sent to collect fire relief money for Stratford in Kent. Two years later—about the time Shakespeare was making out his will—he was accused of failures in accounting for the money he had collected. Was Shakespeare censorious enough at hearing this story to drop Tyler from his will? Whatever the reason, Richard Tyler's name is scratched out and Hamnet Sadler's written in its stead.

It would appear from this ambivalent entry in his will that William Shakespeare and Hamnet Sadler, so close in their youthful days, had drifted apart as their lives changed. Shakespeare, at ease with his many wealthy friends in Stratford, on his return from London found in Hamnet Sadler a man unlucky in business and continually in financial need. Whatever the difficulties the disparity of their fortunes made for them, the will shows that these two boyhood friends stayed connected from the beginning to the very end of Shakespeare's life.

Hamnet Sadler outlived his friend by eight years. He died in 1624, the year after the great First Folio of Shakespeare's plays was published.

Richard Tyler (1566–1636)

Two lads, that thought there was no more behind,
But such a day tomorrow, as today,
And to be boy eternal.

The Winter's Tale, act 1, scene 2

... like a school broke up,
Each hurries toward his home and sporting place.

Henry IV, Part 2, act 4, scene 2

The youngest of Shakespeare's boyhood friends, Richard Tyler, was two years younger than Shakespeare. His footnote in history is secure: he was the legatee crossed out in Shakespeare's will. This unexplained action has given scholars much cause for speculation: Why was his name summarily replaced in the revised will? Why was Hamnet Sadler, the replacement, not in the will from the beginning?

Richard Tyler's father was a butcher and, like John Shakespeare and Adrian Quiney, an alderman on the town council. His son, though we do not know his profession, provides a romantic story not unlike those Shakespeare would later tell in *Two Gentlemen of Verona* and *Romeo and Juliet*. In his book *Shakespeare's Stratford* (p. 39) Edgar Fripp tells us that at age twenty-two Richard Tyler, the son of a butcher, fell in love with Susanna Woodward, eldest daughter of Richard Woodward of nearby Shottery Manor. She was only sixteen. Their run-away marriage so angered her grandfather, Robert Perrott, the wealthy owner of The King's House tavern in Stratford, that he disinherited her. A stern notation in his will warns her sisters to be dutiful and not to marry without their parents' consent.

In the same year as his marriage (1588), Tyler became a soldier, one of the many called up to fight against the mighty Spanish Armada. After taking part in this triumphant victory, Tyler came home to Stratford where he served on the town council from 1590 to 1594, the years Shakespeare was coming to prominence in London. In July of 1598 Tyler's son William was baptized, opening the possibility that Shakespeare was the child's godfather.

In 1607, at forty-one years of age, Richard Tyler was accused of "making affray" with Thomas Lucas, a belligerent and contentious Stratford lawyer. In 1612 Tyler was arrested for breaking the peace, but the town council petitioned for his release, claiming that his accuser was unreliable.

In 1614, after Shakespeare had moved back to Stratford to retire, the town suffered its third devastating fire in ten years. Fifty houses were lost as well as a number of barns storing hay, malt, grain, and timber. The damage was enormous—over 8,000 pounds. Richard Tyler was authorized to go to Kent to seek fire relief funding.

Until this point there was no breach with Shakespeare and his family; the continuing friendship was affirmed when Shakespeare left Tyler money for a memorial ring in his will. However, in 1616, between the first draft of Shakespeare's will in January and the second in March, Richard Tyler was accused of embezzling some of the money he had collected in Kent. In the second draft of the will, Richard

Tyler's name is crossed out and Hamnet Sadler's written in its place. So Shakespeare died, displeased with this boyhood friend.

Richard Tyler remained close to the family, however. In 1618 he signed the deed that transferred the ownership of the Blackfriars Gatehouse, Shakespeare's only London property, from its trustees to Susanna Shakespeare Hall. And his reputation in the town seems to have been reinstated by 1621 when he served as a churchwarden, an office held by his son four years later.

Richard Tyler died in 1636, twenty years after the death of his one-time friend William Shakespeare. He had outlived all the other boyhood friends.

Richard Field (1561–1624)

We turn'd o'er many books together.
The Merchant of Venice, act 4, scene 1

The Fields lived on Bridge Street, a block from the Shakespeares' Henley Street house. Richard Field, born three years before William Shakespeare, was the son of Henry Field, a Stratford tanner and friend of John Shakespeare.

The boys would have known each other since infancy, and in 1579 fifteen-year-old William Shakespeare watched his eighteen-year-old friend set off on an adventure: young Richard was leaving Stratford for the great city of London, where his father had apprenticed him to John Bishop, a printer.

Bishop in turn subcontracted Field to Thomas Vautrollier, a French immigrant who owned a printing business in the precinct of Blackfriars. Field learned printing from Vautrollier during his first five years of apprenticeship, then came home to George Bishop, a specialist in publishing and bookselling.

In 1586 Richard returned to Vautrollier's Blackfriars shop and in 1587, when Vautrollier died, Richard Field not only took over the business but married Vautrollier's widow, Jacqueline (though possibly she was his daughter—the two women had similar names, and C. C. Stopes points out that, as Field's widow kept the business going after his death, she was likely a younger woman than the widow of Vautrollier could have been). Field now owned his own press, and was one of only twenty-two master printers operating in London. A year or so later Shakespeare himself moved to London. How interesting for him to see Richard Field leading his life as a London businessman, and to learn from him about writing and publishing.

Shakespeare might well have seen firsthand the power of government censorship when on May 10, 1589, Field was fined ten shillings for printing a book illegally, or "contrary to order."[8] Over Field's long career the emphasis he placed on printing theological books (about a third of his output) occasionally got him in such trouble with the censors. Ten years later he and his colleagues were called to Stationer's Hall to hear the new and stricter censorship laws emphasized.

On November 3, 1589, Field was also fined two shillings and six pence for keeping an apprentice who was not properly registered. As his was one of the best print shops in London he had, subsequently, many apprentices. They included his younger brother, Jasper, just one of a goodly number of Warwickshire lads who came to London to learn the printer's trade. Jasper arrived in 1592, the year after their father died. The friendship of the Field and Shakespeare families is evident when, after Henry Field's death, his friend John Shakespeare was asked to appraise his goods.

In London the relationship of the sons was particularly close at this time also, for in 1593 and 1594 Richard Field printed Shakespeare's epic poems, *Venus and Adonis* and *The Rape of Lucrece*. These were the only works of his own whose printing Shakespeare himself pursued and supervised. He chose to entrust the poems to his friend Field to print and Field's work was done with such care that they are remarkably free of errors or flaws.

The Fields were living in the Blackfriars area near St. Paul's Cathedral in the late 1500s. In 1596 the end of the documented relationship between Richard Field and William Shakespeare coincides with a petition Richard Field signed with other residents of Blackfriars protesting James Burbage's plan to convert the Blackfriars Theatre—which had been a private theatre for the training of boy actors only—to a public venue for adult professional plays. The protest was driven by a fear that traffic would become unendurable, that the sound of "drums and trumpets" would interrupt services in the nearby church, and that with the collection of undesirables in the neighborhood the theatre would:

> grow to be a very great annoyance and trouble . . . both by reason of the great resort and gathering together of all manner of vagrant and lewd

persons that, under colour of resorting to the plays, will come thither and work all kinds of mischief.[9]

The petition kept the Blackfriars from becoming a professional adult theatre for another decade.

Continued friendly relations between Shakespeare and Richard Field are suggested, however, into the early 1600s, when the Fields were resident in the parish of St. Olave on Wood Street. They lived close to the Mountjoys' house on Silver Street, where Shakespeare moved in about 1602. It is perhaps through the Fields that Shakespeare met the Mountjoys, as the Mountjoys and Mrs. Field were all part of the French Huguenot community.

Richard Field continued his distinguished career to the end of his life. On July 1, 1598, he had been "admitted to the livery"[10] as a servant to the queen and invited to go to the Lord Mayor's Feast. Active in his guild, the Stationers' Company, he helped to draw up their new ordinances in that same year. By 1615 Field owned a new shop, The Splayed Eagle, in Wood Street, where he worked until his death in 1624, having outlived his boyhood friend William Shakespeare by eight years.

Richard Field and William Shakespeare in London

Richard Field was the first and only one of Shakespeare's boyhood friends to settle in London. As Shakespeare set off to take up his new, exciting, and uncertain profession, he knew he would find this one Stratford school friend at the end of the road, a friend who had already broken the ice and was competing successfully in the big city. In addition, Field's trade was directly connected with the work Shakespeare wanted to do.

Biographers who speculate that Shakespeare lived with the Fields for a time observe that the books available in Field's shop constitute a library filled with the information Shakespeare needed as background for his plays. "When we examine the list and nature of Field's publications in these years, we perceive how much they mean in Shakespeare's continued education and reading. For the first book Field printed on his own was Puttenham's *Arte of English Poesie*, the prime Elizabethan work of literary criticism which summed up all that had been achieved in the past thirty years and pointed the way to the future."[11] Other Field publications included pamphlets dealing with French affairs; in these were found descriptions of young men whose names Shakespeare borrowed for *Love's Labours Lost*. The Jacquenetta in that play may be named for Jaqueline Field, who would have been a source for the help Shakespeare needed in writing French dialogue such as that between the princess Katharine, her attendant Alice, and Henry in *Henry V*. The Field-published *Treatise on Melancholy* was a source for *Hamlet*, and his *Campo de Fior* was a popular handbook for learning Italian. This book offered Shakespeare the casual Italian phrases he needed for his early Italian comedies. Field published numerous school texts, including Shakespeare's much-used Ovid, as well as works by Cicero, Plutarch's *Lives*, and Manutius's *Phrases*.

It is astonishing to realize that, had Shakespeare never written a single play, never set foot on a stage, never created a single character, he would still be considered one of the greatest of English Renaissance poets. His reputation would rest where he confidently assumed it would—on the epic poems that Field printed, *Venus and Adonis* (1593) and *The Rape of Lucrece* (1594), and further on his great *Sonnets*—though he would neither have desired nor expected this, as these last were published without his knowledge or permission.

Recognition as a distinguished, published poet was important to Shakespeare early in his career. Distinction for an Elizabethan playwright was no easier to achieve than it is for today's television and advertising writers. And Shakespeare was fortunate in his youthful ambition. By 1592 his reputation was growing among theatregoers and critics alike. His place as a writer and actor and his talent as a poet were so secure that Ian Wilson conjectures persuasively in *Shakespeare, The Evidence* that Henry Wriothesley, the young Earl of Southampton, invited Shakespeare to stay at his house during the plague outbreak of 1592 to 1594. Wilson suggests that it was there that Shakespeare wrote his first great epic poem, *Venus and Adonis*. When Shakespeare finished the poem, he dedicated the work to this new London friend, Southampton, and brought it to his old Stratford friend, Richard Field, for printing.

Field registered *Venus and Adonis* with the Stationers' Company, the guild to which he belonged, which self-policed the industry so that printers and publishers were saved hassle by the government censors. In doing so, Richard Field kept the copyright while he arranged with John Harrison, whose bookstore had the appealing name The White Greyhound, to distribute the book.

Our image of Shakespeare places him constantly onstage at the Globe Theatre, but through Richard Field he became equally acquainted with the busy, crowded, competitive life of the London book trade. When he resided in Blackfriars, Shakespeare lived two blocks from street after street of printers' shops, publishers' offices, and bookstores.

Churches were the center of manuscript writing in the Middle Ages, so as printing came into being, presses and bookstores clustered around great cathedrals. In Renaissance London, St. Paul's Cathedral marked the center of the book trade. It was not the cathedral we know today with its great dome by Christopher Wren, but rather the crumbling remains of a great gothic church as beautiful and dominating as Notre Dame in Paris. The interior, however, was gutted by Henry VIII during his dissolution of the monasteries, and the great spire that reached 465 feet (100 feet taller than St. Paul's dome) was struck by lightning and destroyed in 1560. Determined to rid the country of papist reminders, Henry had watched over the destruction of stained-glass windows, statuaries representing saints, stations of the cross, and other Roman Catholic symbols. While Anglican services still took place in the sanctuary, the book business and other commercial enterprises encroached on the space in the denuded great nave and stretched out into the cathedral close, making St. Paul's a pedestrian crossroads and a place of commerce and public meetings.

As Shakespeare strode along Paternoster Row, the street running along the north side of the cathedral and Blackfriars just to the southwest, he saw dozens of bookshops two and three stories high. Built in the familiar half-timbered Tudor style, their second and third stories cantilevered out over the street. Colorful names and decorative signs called out: "White Horse," "Bishop's Head," "Brazen Serpent," "Green Dragon," "Three Pigeons"—among many more.

Elizabethans were voracious readers. These bookstores promoted and sold religious books such as the Bible and the Book of Common Prayer, sermons, and doctrinal tracts. They offered law books, schoolbooks, translations of classic works, books covering history, music, and literature, in addition to broadsides, pamphlets, ballads, and proclamations. Readers ranged from the barely literate to the university-educated.

In *A Companion to Shakespeare*, David Scott Kastan offers several chapters on printing in the time of Shakespeare. Within Kastan's book Mark Bland points out that eighty percent of the libraries of Ben Jonson and John Donne were published on the Continent[12] and represent just some of the many books available in foreign languages, while Laurie E. Maguire indicates that bookstores' advertising included the printing of many copies of a book's title page to post where they would be seen by passersby. The crassness of this practice so offended Ben Jonson that he forbade his publisher to adopt it.[13] We have no record of Shakespeare being so sensitive.

Though many plays were published, play scripts did not make a lot of money for the writer or for the publisher. Poetry like *Venus and Adonis* did. Shakespeare's success with that work was followed by the even greater success of *The Rape of Lucrece*, which had four editions in six years and from which an anthology at the end of the century cited ninety-one quotations.

Interestingly, though Field had been the chosen publisher for *Venus and Adonis*, it was John Harrison, the owner of The White Greyhound Bookstore, who registered *The Rape of Lucrece* with the Stationer's Guild and thus held the copyright. Harrison hired Field to print *The Rape of Lucrece*. He then got Field to transfer the copyright of *Venus and Adonis* to him. Harrison was the more prestigious publisher, but one wonders what the ramifications of this transaction were on the friendship between Field and Shakespeare. Something happened between them, for Shakespeare makes no mention of Field in his will. Richard Quiney predeceased Field, and the other boyhood friends, Richard Tyler and Hamnet Sadler, are mentioned in Shakespeare's will. But before Shakespeare died, his friendship with Richard Field had faded.

The year 1594 was a turning point in Shakespeare's life. After *The Rape of Lucrece*, he wrote no more epic poetry. Obviously he could have. He could at that point in time have changed his life completely and given himself over to the serious poetry which would gain him aristocratic patronage, fame, and artistic distinction. But Shakespeare walked away from his early friends the Fields, and from the bustling crooked streets around St. Paul's, filled with print shops and books. He turned his back on a literary life and strode back across town to Shoreditch Road, to Finsbury Fields, and to the theatre. He chose to join the Lord Chamberlain's Men, and his friends who were its owners and its managers, its writers and its actors.

The Combe Family

William Combe (1551–1610)
John Combe (c. 1561–1614) (nephew of William)
Thomas Combe (?–1609) (nephew of William)

Thomas Combe (1589–1657) (son of Thomas)
William Combe (1586–1667) (son of Thomas)

If any man ask who lies in this tomb
"O, ho," quoth the devil, " 'Tis my John-a-Combe."
Epitaph attributed to Shakespeare

In his will Shakespeare left his sword to twenty-seven-year-old Thomas Combe. It is a poignant bequest, as the sword was the kind of personal item Shakespeare might have left his son Hamnet had the boy lived. The young men might have been friends, for they would have been close in age and the families lived nearby and shared a long history. In any event, the sword was an appropriate bequest, for Thomas Combe possessed a bellicose nature.

The Combes were a wealthy family of landowners and lawyers and Shakespeare's friendship with them was close especially after his retirement to Stratford around 1611. Shakespeare's contemporary, Thomas Combe, died in 1609, his brother John in 1614. Nephew William was the heir to all their property and took action almost immediately to claim, by enclosing them, the common fields of Welcombe (just outside Stratford). When the Stratford Council objected to this appropriation of public lands, younger brother Thomas (the inheritor of Shakespeare's sword) accused them of being dogs and curs, while William called them "Puritan knaves and underlings."[14]

Shakespeare was dragged into the controversy as he had invested in tithes that included some of the contested property. The Combes' agent assured Shakespeare's agent and friend, the Stratford clerk Thomas Greene, that they would compensate Shakespeare for any loss to his tithes. Greene reported on November 17, 1614, "my cousin Shakespeare coming yesterday to town, I went to see him how he did. He told me that they assured him they meant to enclose no further than to the Gospel Bush and so up straight, leaving out part of the dingles . . . and that they mean in April to survey the land, and then to give satisfaction and not before. And he and Master Hall say they think there will be nothing done at all."[15] Greene further noted in a diary entry: "I also writ of myself to my cousin Shakespeare the copies of all our oaths made then, also a note of the inconveniences would grow by the enclosure." No response survives from Shakespeare.

Tenants, alarmed at the enclosure of these heretofore common fields, filled in the ditches the Combes had dug and tried to cut down the hedges. When Combe's men threw the protestors to the ground,

William Combe "sat laughing on horseback and said they were good football players."[16] The conflict worsened as supporters from Stratford and Bishopton raced to help fill the ditches and tear down the mounds. Even when a judge ruled against the enclosure, William Combe continued to harass and imprison his tenants—perhaps taking advantage of his position as Sheriff of Warwickshire (1615–1616). In September, Thomas Greene noted: "Master Shakespeare's telling J. Greene [Thomas Greene's brother and deputy town clerk] that he was not able to bear the enclosing of Welcombe."[17]

The contentious young pair William and Thomas were more than twenty years younger than Shakespeare. His closer friendship was with their uncle John Combe, a landowner, moneylender, and the richest citizen in Stratford. John, along with his Uncle William, a member of Parliament who lived in nearby Warwick, sold Shakespeare 127 acres of land in Stratford in 1602.

The buying, selling, leasing of property, and other legal actions give us most of the records that document Shakespeare's life. From them we get the names of numerous acquaintances and friends. The Belott-Mountjoy legal suit, the Blackfriars Gatehouse purchase, various land and housing purchases in Stratford, and lawsuits over taxes and tithes put the reclusive Shakespeare's name into public record and often brought Shakespeare into contact with his lawyer friends. In addition, birth, marriage, and burial records, Shakespeare's will, and the wills of his friends give us valuable and often tantalizing information.

John Combe was a bachelor, perhaps unaware that leaving his property to his nephew William would trigger civil dissent. His more benign bequests included twenty pounds to the poor of Stratford and five pounds to his friend William Shakespeare. Combe lies in Trinity Church, Stratford, and his monument was designed by Gheerart Janssen, who designed Shakespeare's monument two years later.

Legend has it that before John Combe's death Shakespeare did "fan up some witty and facetious verses" for Combe's epitaph:

> Ten in the hundred lies here engraved,
> 'Tis a hundred to ten, his soul is not saved,
> If any man ask who lies in this tomb
> "O, ho," quoth the devil, " 'Tis my John-a-Combe."[18]

If attribution of this doggerel to Shakespeare seems unlikely, Nicholas Burgh, who calls himself a Poor Knight of Windsor in a manuscript from 1650, claims that

Mr. Ben Jonson and Mr. Wm. Shakespeare being merry at a tavern, Mr. Jonson having begun this for his epitaph: "Here lies Ben Jonson that was once one," he gives it to Mr. Shakespeare to make up who presently writes:
> "Who while he live'd was a slow thing
> And now being dead is nothing."[19]

These anecdotes indicate an attractive jocular spirit as Shakespeare and his friends faced their mortality. The accounts are evidence of Shakespeare's willingness to toss off light-hearted verse. Or perhaps they just reveal a desire of Shakespeare's admirers to hang onto these ill-documented, apocryphal tales out of a need to see the genial author in a more human light.

If the legend is true, the playful epitaph did not seem to offend John Combe, as witness his bequest to Shakespeare in his will. In contrast to the impecunious Hamnet Sadler, the Combes were on a high social and economic level, one comfortable to Shakespeare in the years of his retirement. They were active, successful politicians and lawyers, wealthy landowners, and important public figures in the hometown to which Shakespeare returned at the end of his life. The upheaval caused by the younger generation, though distressing to Shakespeare, did not keep him from leaving his sword (perhaps with his ever present sense of ironic humor) to contentious young Thomas Combe.

The Nash Family

Anthony Nash ?–1622
John Nash ?–1623
Thomas Nash 1593–1647 (son of Anthony)

We few, we happy few, we band of brothers.
Henry V, act 4, scene 3

John and Anthony Nash (variously spelled with and without a final "e") were two brothers, each of whom was left two marks in Shakespeare's will with which to buy rings. Anthony helped farm Shakespeare's land and manage his tithes, and was called upon three times to witness papers for Shakespeare: in 1602 (for the purchase of property from the Combes, illustrating that friendships in small Stratford crisscrossed in many patterns), and also in 1603 and 1614. A wealthy man, he left more than 1,000 pounds plus property to his son Thomas, who continued to play a role in the Shakespeare family story.

John Nash, with his second wife Dorothy, took possession of and ran her late husband's Bear Inn on Bridge Street in Stratford. Another one of "gentle" Shakespeare's friends of bellicose temperament, Nash objected to the Puritanism of the vicar appointed to Trinity Church in Stratford. He led a riot against the new vicar in 1619 (three years after Shakespeare's death and just four years before his own). The rioters' outrage led them to threaten to flay the vicar alive in his own church, for which they (including John Nash) were sued in Star Chamber.

As with other close Stratford associates, the Nash/Shakespeare friendship spanned generations. Thomas, John's nephew and Anthony's son, married Shakespeare's granddaughter Elizabeth Hall in 1626 when he was thirty-three and she eighteen. He was a lawyer, having entered Lincoln's Inn in 1616, but he never needed to practice law as he inherited a great deal of money, two houses, land from his father Anthony, and the Bear Inn from his Uncle John.

Born in 1593, Thomas Nash was twenty-three when Shakespeare died (whereas Elizabeth was only eight, with marriage well in the future for the little girl). So Shakespeare knew Thomas in the prime of his early manhood, and Thomas must often have thought of old William Shakespeare as he and his young wife took up residence in Nash House, next door to her late grandfather Shakespeare's New Place.

In November 1635 Thomas Nash's father-in-law Dr. John Hall died, leaving Nash his "study of books."[20] As Susanna Shakespeare, Hall's wife, was Shakespeare's primary legatee, this "study" must have included whichever of Shakespeare's own books Susanna chose not to keep.

When Anthony Nash died at the age of fifty-three in 1647 he was buried in the chancel of Trinity Church, Stratford, just to the right of Shakespeare, with the arms of Nash, Hall, and Shakespeare carved on his gravestone.

William Reynolds (1575–1633)

Maria: Marry, sir, sometimes he is a kind of puritan.
Andrew: O, if I thought that, I'd beat him like a dog.

Twelfth Night, act 2, scene 3

William Reynolds was another recipient of a two-marks-for-a-ring bequest in Shakespeare's will. The Reynolds family comprised twenty-two persons, counting the servants, and was the largest household in Stratford. They lived four houses from Shakespeare's New Place (just past the Nashes' house and the house of Julian Shaw) and, in addition, owned a farm near Trinity Church. Committed Catholics, the Reynolds chose to pay heavy fines to avoid going to Church of England services. Furthermore, William Reynolds' recusant parents had sheltered a fleeing Jesuit priest, and his mother Margaret was one of those accused with Susanna Shakespeare of not receiving communion on Easter 1606. They were not unduly punished, however, and the next year Susanna married a thoroughly Protestant man, Dr. John Hall.

So we come around again to the question of Shakespeare and religion. His private thoughts on the matter remain well hidden. Speculation comes up against the fact that he never failed to comply with approved observances, and his friendships transcended religious beliefs: though a number of his Stratford friends, like the Reynolds family and perhaps like his own father, clung to the old Catholic beliefs, his wife, son-in-law, and daughter were connected with the rising Puritan tide.

William Reynolds' Catholic feelings ran deep. Along with John Nash he was charged in Star Chamber with rioting against the "sucking Puritans of Stratford" and threatening to flay in the church the Puritan vicar who replaced easy-going John Rogers. Reynolds came under suspicion for being a hidden Catholic when a maypole was said to have been set up near his house. This was in 1619, three years after Shakespeare's death, and is evidence of how puritanical the town had become by the end of his life. Reynolds escaped punishment, however, became a large landowner in Old Stratford, and lived until 1633.

Thomas Greene (c. 1578–1641)

...I commit into your hands
The husbandry and manage of my house.
                    The Merchant of Venice, act 3, scene 4

From 1609 to 1611 Shakespeare's family in Stratford shared their home with the family of a man who identified himself as Shakespeare's cousin: Thomas Greene. Born in 1578, Greene was fourteen years younger than

Shakespeare. He was a lawyer who matriculated at the Middle Temple in 1595, sponsored in part by the dramatist John Marston, a man barely three years his elder. Marston was deeply involved in the same theatrical circles as Shakespeare, as he wrote plays for the Admiral's Men and the boys of St. Paul's, worked with Dekker, and fulminated against Ben Jonson with whom he later became friends. Shakespeare's friendship with Greene, and Greene's with Marston, indicate a likelihood that Shakespeare and Marston were also well acquainted. A precocious young man, Greene seems not to have been tempted by the theatrical world. He took his law degree and became solicitor for Stratford in 1601 when he was only twenty-three. From 1603 to 1617 he was town clerk and represented Stratford in London as town counsel.

Whether a familial "cousin" or a friendly "cousin" (evidence of familial connections has not been found), Thomas Greene had a very close relationship with William Shakespeare. Greene named his children Anne and William. He and his family were invited to live with Shakespeare's family from 1609–1611 while Greene's house near the church was being made ready to receive him. The house the Greene and Shakespeare families shared was New Place.

Purchased May 4, 1597, New Place was the second-largest house in Stratford. Sixty feet long, it was made of rosy brick and had leaded windows, ten chimneys, and a bow window looking out on the garden. Furthermore, the property included two barns and two orchards. Records from 1614 show one occasion when sack and claret were ordered at New Place to be served to a preacher, but no other signs of lavish hospitality exist. Entertainment aside, with the ownership of this glorious house came high social status in Stratford. Shakespeare, as owner of New Place, possessed a special pew in the church called Clopton Pew, named for the builder of New Place, Sir Hugh Clopton, whose bridge across the Avon still bears his name. Among New Place's several residents was one of Henry VIII's physicians.

In July of 1605 Shakespeare spent 440 pounds to purchase an interest in the tithes on corn and other crops from property located in Old Stratford, Bishopton, and Welcombe—a large and relatively secure investment. Anthony Nash was a witness to this purchase, and Shakespeare's lawyer who drew up and witnessed the deed was Francis Collins, the same lawyer who would write Shakespeare's will eleven years later.

In 1614 a crisis concerning this investment gives us some treasured documentation on Shakespeare's life, whereabouts, and relationship to Thomas Greene. A man named Arthur Mainwaring, along with William Combe, decided on the death of John Combe to enclose the public fields at Welcombe. The town's response to this action was emotional and violent. Shakespeare's reaction was tempered by the assurance of the Combes' agent that any loss to those owning tithes would be compensated. Thomas Greene, as town clerk of Stratford, drew up the papers summarizing Shakespeare's interest. In the papers referring to the enclosures, Thomas Green twice refers to "my cousin Shakespeare." One of the papers, dated November 17, 1614, refers to Shakespeare's coming to London and describes the personal conversation Greene had with Shakespeare and Mr. Hall (Shakespeare's physician son-in-law) when Greene "went to see him how he did."[21] Shakespeare described the fields Combe meant to enclose, and noted that he and his son-in-law thought the enclosing might not happen after all because of the limitations on Combe. It took the uprising of the townsfolk and their filling in Combe's ditches to make William Combe admit defeat.

Throughout these events Shakespeare took the calm and prudent course, staying home at New Place. Unfortunately, this incident seems to have created a breech between Shakespeare and his longtime friend Thomas Greene. Within two years Shakespeare would be making his will in which the Greenes, after so many years of close friendship, were not mentioned. And Shakespeare's large Stratford home that the families shared no longer stands. Only the brick wall and the beautiful garden remain to inspire us with the memory of the man who walked its paths with his own family, and who once, with Thomas Greene and his little William and Anne, wandered the lawn and enjoyed its flowers four hundred years ago.

John Hall (1575–1635)

This disease is beyond my practice.

Macbeth, act 5, scene 1

Shakespeare died on April 23, 1616, undoubtedly attended by his son-in-law, Dr. John Hall. Married to Shakespeare's beloved eldest daughter Susanna, Hall was the most distinguished physician in the Stratford area, so Shakespeare had the best care available. But his disease was beyond even Hall's practice and Shakespeare died at the age of fifty-two.

John Hall is typical of the friends of Shakespeare's maturity: well educated, professional, and highly successful. Born in 1575, he was just eleven years younger than Shakespeare. His father, William Hall, was a physician from Acton, a village in Middlesex. John Hall was born at Carlton in Bedfordshire, went to Cambridge with his brother Dive in 1589, and was granted both a B.A. (1594) and an M.A. (1597) from Queen's College. Though Hall received neither a degree nor a license in medicine, his father left him all of his medical books when he died. Another doctor of the time, James Cooke, who observed that Hall spoke French well, raised the possibility that John Hall had studied medicine in one of the French universities, such as Montpellier, which was known for its medical school. Whatever his training, John Hall seems to have had no trouble setting up practice in Stratford at the turn of the seventeenth century, though why he chose this particular town is unknown.

Hall's Croft in Stratford illustrates how a doctor of the time lived and practiced medicine. When Susanna Shakespeare left the elegant home her father had provided at New Place, she moved into an equally commodious two-story, honey-colored house. The doctor's family lived in ease, their rooms comfortable and airy, heated by large fireplaces in the winter and filled with light from a number of windows. The house combined living and business areas. Hall employed two apothecaries, one of whom concocted and dispensed medicines from a small room in the house, and whose prescriptions (or "bills") were often made from herbs grown in the adjacent garden. The doctor visited patients in their own homes, however. He would not have been eager to have diseases brought into his home by sick patients, and transporting severely ill people was neither easy nor practical. Those who could not afford the doctor's consultation, or who could not wait for his visit, could receive advice and medicines directly from the apothecaries.

John Hall's house calls took him far afield to Burford and Worcester where he treated the Bishop for scurvy, a treatment consisting of his own "Scorbutick beer" made from sweetened ale mixed with herbs. He treated the poet Michael Drayton and Drayton's patrons Sir Henry and Lady Anne Rainsford in nearby Clifford Chambers, as well as the Earl and Countess of Northampton who lived at Ludlow Castle forty miles away.

Physicians and surgeons practicing outside London were subject to periodic visitations by the bishop of London or his representative, to whom they had to present their licenses. In 1622 the visitation came to Stratford and the town's three other practicing physicians appeared, but John Hall was excused.

In 1614 John Hall accompanied his father-in-law on a trip to London. As was the case with so many of his other friends, Shakespeare's personality contrasted with John Hall's. Introspective, "gentle," and noncombative Shakespeare rode next to a man of strong Protestant-puritanical leanings (as Marchette Chute quotes: "such who spare not for cost, and they who have more than ordinary understanding—nay such as hated him for his religion often made use of him"[22]). John Hall was a man who would refuse knighthood in 1626, and when he ran out of excuses for being too busy to serve on the town council in 1632, he attended meetings only sporadically. When he did attend, the meetings were marked by "continual disturbances." How did this scientist, physician, and churchwarden (1628–1629) with Puritan sympathies come to terms with a father-in-law who had made his fortune in a profession condemned as satanic by the Puritans of the day?

Come to terms he did. In 1616 John and Susanna Hall returned to London on the sad journey to prove Shakespeare's will, for which they were named executors. And it is likely, since Judith Shakespeare could not have afforded it, that the Halls commissioned Gheerart Janssen to design the monument that marks Shakespeare's final resting place in Trinity Church. The Halls were left New Place and moved there, into Shakespeare's beloved home, to live until they died. A contrast in personality it seems did not keep John Hall and William Shakespeare from being trusted friends.

John Hall kept a diary, or casebook. In this diary he detailed in Latin 178 of his patients' complaints (including his own, his wife's, and his daughter's) and how he cured them. From this diary we know that in 1624 his daughter, Shakespeare's granddaughter Elizabeth, went to London, and that soon after she came back she came down with a cold and *tortura oris* (convulsion of the mouth), which he cured:

> In the beginning of April she went to London and returning homewards the 22nd of the said month she took cold and fell into the said distemper on the contrary side of the face...and although grievously afflicted by it, yet by the blessing of God she was cured in sixteen days, as followeth...the neck was fomented with *aqua vitae*, in which was infused nutmegs, cinnamon, cloves, pepper; she ate nutmegs often. In the same year, May the 24th, she was afflicted with an erratic fever: sometimes she was hot, by and by sweating, again cold, all in the space of half an hour, and thus was she vexed oft in a day...thus was she delivered from death and deadly disease, and was well for many years.[23]

The above account is from the translation from Latin into English by Warwickshire surgeon James Cooke who believed John Hall's casebooks to be of such importance that he published a translation in 1657 titled *Select Observations on English Bodies*. Unfortunately for us, only the second volume has been found and the earliest entry in it is dated 1617. If we had the first volume, we might have known the cause of Shakespeare's death. But Shakespeare became ill one year too soon to be included in volume two, and we have no information from his physician about his final days.

Shakespeare portrays doctors who have impressive sympathy in both *Macbeth* and *King Lear*. A special sensitivity to the connection between mind and body pervades the doctors' language as they observe the madness of Lady Macbeth and encourage the waking of the comatose King Lear. Shakespeare wrote these plays between 1603 and 1606, well after John Hall's arrival in Stratford around 1600. Hall had become close to the Shakespeare family about that time, as he married Susanna Shakespeare on June 5, 1607. That same year Shakespeare was working on *Pericles*, where there appears a nobleman and physician named Cerimon. His exchange with the 2nd Gentleman in act 3, scene 2 might be a portrait of John Hall:

> Cerimon
>   'Tis known, I ever
> Have studied physic, through which secret art,
> By turning o'er authorities, I have,
> Together with my practice, made familiar
> To me and to my aid the blest infusions
> That dwell in vegetatives, in metals, stones;
> And I can speak of the disturbances
> That nature works, and of her cures; which doth give me
> A more content in course of true delight
> Than to be thirsty after tottering honour,
> Or tie my treasure up in silken bags,
> To please the fool and death.
>
> 2nd Gentleman
> Your honour has through Ephesus poured forth
> Your charity, and hundreds call themselves
> Your creatures, who by you have been restored;
> And not your knowledge, your personal pain, but even

Your purse, still open, hath built Lord Cerimon
Such strong renown as time shall never raze.

At his death in 1635, John Hall left goods and money worth over a thousand pounds to be divided between his wife Susanna and daughter Elizabeth, who by this time had married Thomas Nash. To Thomas Nash, who lived with Elizabeth next door to the Halls at New Place, Hall left all his books.

John Hall and his wife Susanna are buried near William Shakespeare in Holy Trinity Church, Stratford. His epitaph indicates the esteem in which he was held:

Johannes Hall, medicus peritissimus
Heere lyeth ye Body of John Hall, gent:
hee marr: Susanna, ye daughter, & coheire of Will: Shakespeare, gent.
Hee deceased nover: 25. A. 1635, aged 60.
Hallius hic situs est medica celeberrimus arte;
Expectans regni Gaudia laeta Dei;
Dignus erat meritis, qui nestora vinceret annis;
In terris omnes, sed rapit aequa dies.
Ne tumulo, quid desit adest fidessima coniux,
Et vitae comitem nunc quoque mortis habet.[24]

[Here lies Hall, most celebrated for the physician's art
Awaiting the joys of the Kingdom of God;
He was worthy of reward, he who vied with Nestor's years,
Throughout all lands; but was taken by the day that takes us all.
That his tomb may lack nothing, his most faithful wife
Is here, his companion in life, now his companion in death.]

Thomas Russell (1570–1634)

Have to my widow!
                    The Taming of the Shrew, act 5, scene 1

Thomas Russell was one of the overseers of Shakespeare's will and Shakespeare left him a bequest of five pounds. A lawyer, Russell was educated at Queen's College, Oxford, which he entered in 1588 at the age of eighteen. His second marriage connected him to Shakespeare. His first wife, whom he married in 1590, and both his little daughters by her, died within the decade. After these great tragedies, he wooed Anne Digges, a widow who lived in Aldermanbury, the London parish where the three friends Henry Condell, John Heminges, and William Shakespeare were her neighbors.

The Russell-Digges romance must have intrigued the neighborhood. Anne Digges's first husband, Thomas, was a brilliant mathematician and astronomer who wrote two books which were the first to explain the Copernican system to English readers. Much of his other writing on ballistics, navigation, ship design, and the like, was left unfinished because he involved himself in endless lawsuits. As a member of Parliament, Digges was accounted one of the most eloquent debaters in the House of Commons. When he died in 1595 his will prevented Anne from inheriting if she married again.

Not to be thwarted, Anne Digges and Thomas Russell lived together, betrothed but unmarried, while she set herself to contest the will. At stake was the great fortune of twelve thousand pounds. When, after two years' struggle, she was successful, Anne Digges married Thomas Russell. But her son Dudley, another remarkable politician and supporter of exploration who had inherited his father's litigious personality, brought suit to contest her breaking of the trust. The litigation between Dudley and Anne Digges is filled with abusive language toward Thomas Russell. This is a pity, as Thomas Russell seems a generous man: he helped the family of his friend John Hanford, and with Hanford, contributed to buy new organs for Worcester Cathedral.

Russell had wanted to buy Clopton House near Stratford, which, like New Place, had been built by Hugh Clopton or his family. This would have made him Shakespeare's near neighbor. But the sale fell through, and he subsequently purchased the lease of Rushock Manor near Droitwich.

Anne Digges's family included a daughter, Ursula, and a second son, Leonard, who provides another connection to Shakespeare. Leonard Digges graduated from University College, Oxford, and lived his adult life in that city. He was an author who specialized in translations of French and especially Spanish literature. In 1623, on the occasion of the publication of the First Folio of Shakespeare's plays by his mother's former neighbors Heminges and Condell (and again in 1640), Leonard Digges wrote verses praising Shakespeare:

> Shakespeare, at length thy pious fellowes give
> The world thy works, thy workes, by which, outlive

Thy tombe, thy name must: when that stone is rent
And time dissolves thy Stratford Moniment,
Here we alive shall view thee still...
Be sure, our Shakespeare, thou canst never die,
But crowned with laurel, live eternally.[25]

Shakespeare traveled little but read widely. One wonders if through Leonard Digges Shakespeare came to know the great works of the Spanish literature of the Golden Age. Leonard Digges's first book was published a year after Shakespeare died, but Shakespeare might have conversed with him about Cervantes. Shakespeare might have had his imagination fired by images of Don Quixote and Sancho Panza, or known of the plays of his contemporary, the prodigious Lope de Vega, because Thomas Russell and Anne and Leonard Digges were his friends.

Alexander Aspinall (c. 1546–1624)

O, thou monster Ignorance, how deformed dost thou look!
Love's Labour's Lost, act 4, scene 2

I'll but bring my young man here to school. Look where his master comes.
The Merry Wives of Windsor, act 4, scene 1

Alexander Aspinall became master of Stratford Grammar School in 1582. He remained in that post until he died in 1624, having served a long term of forty-two years. Though he arrived too late to teach William Shakespeare, he schooled Shakespeare's younger brothers Richard and Edmund. Some think Aspinall was the inspiration for Holofernes, the pedant in *Love's Labour's Lost*. But Holofernes is a caricature of a pedant, whereas Aspinall was a respected and distinguished member of Stratford society.

Aspinall was a graduate of Brasenose College, Oxford (1572–1575) and bore the nickname "Great Philip of Macedon."[26] When he first came to Stratford from Lancaster he lived in the Schoolmaster's Chamber in the Guild Hall; later he moved to the Old School.

Like Shakespeare's father, but atypical for a schoolmaster, he was active in city politics, becoming a burgess, alderman (1602), chamberlain, head-borough for Shakespeare's ward, and deputy town clerk (1613), during which service he often kept the council minutes. He never wanted to be bailiff, for he seemed content with service on the council. His peers kept him on for "his continual advice and great experience in the borough affairs...and in regard he is an ancient Master of Art, and a man learned."[27]

His entry into town politics followed his second marriage. In 1594, at the age of forty-eight and long a widower, he courted Ann Shaw, the widow of Ralph Shaw, and heir to her husband's wool business. With their marriage Aspinall became a businessman as well as a teacher, active in buying and selling malt.

Aspinall gave Ann a pair of gloves as a courtship present. The Shaws were longtime neighbors of the Shakespeares in Henley Street, so these gloves were likely made by Shakespeare's father. Aspinall sent the gloves to Ann with the poem:

> The gift is small
> The will is all
> Alexander Aspinall[28]

Half a century later Sir Francis Fane, of Bulbeck recorded in his commonplace book that the poem was by "Shaxpaire upon a pair of gloves that master sent to his mistress." As with the doggerel epitaph for John Combe, there is no proof, but much delight, in attributing to Shakespeare these inconsequential verses celebrating the lives of his friends.

Alexander Aspinall, eighteen years Shakespeare's senior, is the only academic we find among Shakespeare's friends. The ease with which Aspinall moved from the scholastic world into business and political circles must be in part a reason for this friendship. He shared the diversity of Shakespeare's interests and his comfort level in the various worlds of writing, reading, acting, management, real estate, and business.

Julius Shaw (1571–1629)

Thou art a fellow of a good respect;
Thy life hath had some snatch of honour in it.

Julius Caesar, act 5, scene 5

There were five witnesses to Shakespeare's will: Francis Collins, his lawyer; Hamnet Sadler, his childhood friend; John Robinson, likely his tenant in the Blackfriars Gatehouse, London; Robert Whatcott, about whom little is known except that he acted as a character witness for Susanna Shakespeare in her action for slander against Ralph Lane; and Julius Shaw, a near neighbor and high bailiff of Stratford.

Julius (or July) Shaw was Alexander Aspinall's stepson, Anne Shaw's son from her marriage to Ralph Shaw. He lived on Chapel Street, two doors down from New Place, next door to the Nashes. Julius Shaw was married to Anne Boyes and his prosperity came from trading in wool and building materials that he provided to the Corporation (to which he was elected in 1603).

Like his stepfather, Julius Shaw was active in town politics: he was elected alderman in 1613 and had served as a churchwarden and chamberlain. He was spoken of as honest and faithful, and when he was called upon to witness Shakespeare's will he had risen to become high bailiff.

John Robinson (fl. c. 1616)

> In the name of God, Amen. I, William Shakespeare . . . in perfect
> health and memory, God be praised, do make and ordain this
> my last will and testament in manner and form following.
> William Shakespeare's will

John Robinson, the witness to Shakespeare's will, has most often been thought to be the John Robinson, laborer, listed in Stratford records for the baptisms of two sons (1589 and 1605) and two marriages (1579 and 1609), and listed three times as a plaintiff in the local courts. The 1605 baptismal record lists his occupation as "labourer." However, in *Shakespeare the Evidence* Ian Wilson makes a persuasive argument in favor of the witness to the will being John Robinson the tenant of Shakespeare's only London property, the Blackfriars Gatehouse ("the Blackfriars in London near the Wardrobe . . . in wherein one John Robinson dwelleth"[29]).

A John Robinson worked as the steward to the master of the Royal Wardrobe, which was located very near the Blackfriars Gatehouse. This was likely the same John Robinson who signed the Blackfriars residents' 1596 petition against James Burbage's plan to turn the Blackfriars into a professional theatre. This Robinson is also likely to be the man to whom Shakespeare leased his only London property.

John Robinson was such a common name that a positive identification is impossible. But according to both Ian Wilson and Robert Payne, John Robinson's signature on the will looks like that of an educated man, not a laborer. Furthermore, Wilson points out that only three witnesses were needed for the will, so there was no need to find the local John Robinson just because another signature was necessary.

If the John Robinson witnessing the will was Shakespeare's tenant, he was (once again, as noted by Wilson) the only one of Shakespeare's London friends to have been at Shakespeare's side when he died. Shakespeare's last represented London connection was therefore not a work colleague, nor a sentimental companion, but a business associate.

Francis Collins (?–1617)

But here's a parchment...
I found it in his closet, 'tis his will.

Julius Caesar, act 3, scene 2

How did Shakespeare die? In all probability he was at home surrounded by his family (Anne, his wife; his daughters Susanna and Judith; his granddaughter Elizabeth) and cared for by Susanna's husband, the noted physician Dr. John Hall. Shakespeare was only fifty-two, not an advanced age, even at that time. The month was April, the day the twenty-third—the same day on which it is thought he was born. He had made a will in January; then, in March, he revised it.

The solicitor who drew up the will was Francis Collins, a man who, in a way, brings us closer to Shakespeare than any other individual, for this document contains Shakespeare's last earthly wishes, dictated directly to Francis Collins by Shakespeare.

Shakespeare's will is the longest and most tantalizing document we have concerning Shakespeare's life. No final, clean copy seems to have been made. The three pages are of different sizes, a number of the words are blotted; the month, "Januarii," is crossed out at the top and "Martii" (March) is written instead; the revisions were interpolated into the earlier will and Shakespeare signed it in three places: in the middle of the third sheet, in the margin of the first page, and on the bottom of the second sheet.

It is thought that, because of the timing of the writing of the will and its approximation to his death, Shakespeare was suffering from a debilitating illness. However, the will opens with the words

> In the name of God, Amen. I, William Shakespeare . . . in perfect health and memory, God be praised, do make and ordain this my last will and testament in manner and form following.[30]

There was a second common form used to begin a will which states that the maker is "sick of body but of good and perfect memory (God be praised)." The use of the first form leads Marchette Chute to think that Shakespeare was not ill. However, Ian Wilson notes that the form was the same one Collins had used to make John Combe's will three years before and use of it merely indicated a preference for a standard formulation. Some lawyers, it seemed, preferred the "perfect health and memory" stipulation regardless of the state of their clients.

The revision of the will was determined, at least in part, by the marriage of Shakespeare's younger daughter, Judith, and reveals Shakespeare's displeasure with the match. Judith Shakespeare married Thomas Quiney on February 10, 1616. She was thirty-one, he was twenty-seven. A thirty-one-year-old spinster of the time might understandably be thrilled to have any husband at all, but Thomas Quiney was not a great catch. On March 12, 1616, Quiney was temporarily excommunicated by the church for not having obtained a special licence to marry during Lent. Further, he had impregnated a local woman named Margaret Wheeler. She died giving birth to their child on March 15, and ten days later, on March 25, Shakespeare changed his will—this was the same day Quiney was to appear before the ecclesiastical court to confess to the sin of "carnal copulation."

Shakespeare's older daughter Susanna was the main beneficiary of the will. His bequests to Judith are decidedly limited: a bowl of gilded silver, plus 150 pounds and the promise of another 150 if she or a child was living at the end of three years—and that only if she is married and "such husband" assures her land "answerable to the portion." Shakespeare evidently did not trust Judith's husband, though he was the son of his old friend.

The dry, formulaic will does not include affectionate references to his family and its basic provisions are standard for the time. Much has been made of his leaving his wife Anne the "second-best bed." However, it is assumed that the best bed was for guests, so leaving his wife the second-best indicated that she would be assured of keeping their own conjugal bed and that she would undoubtedly live out her life in the family house with her daughter Susanna. Sparing his elderly wife difficulty, the will clearly indicates Shakespeare's desire that Susanna be in charge of his estate after his death.

The will is a major source of knowledge about Shakespeare's friends. Those named include overseers Thomas Russell and Francis Collins; the witnesses were Francis Collins, July (Julius) Shaw, John Robinson, Hamnet Sadler, and Robert Whatcott; the executors were Susanna and John Hall (Shakespeare's daughter and son-in-law). Among his friends, Shakespeare leaves bequests to Thomas Combe, Thomas Russell, Francis Collins, Hamnet Sadler, William Reynolds, Anthony and John Nash, and William Walker. He mentions only three friends from London, so they must have been those closest to him: John Heminges, Richard Burbage, and Henry Condell.

No birth date is known for Francis Collins. During most of his adult life he lived in Warwick, but he was appointed steward to the Corporation of Stratford on April 8, 1616, just before Shakespeare's death, and moved to Stratford at that time. He died the following year.

During the writing and revision of Shakespeare's will, Francis Collins, an old friend and the lawyer who had assisted Shakespeare with legal documents throughout his life, sat with Shakespeare. He listened to Shakespeare's voice, observed his decline in health, advised him, heard his desires, recorded them, evaluated his relationship with his family members and friends, and at the last, as Shakespeare signed his will, Francis Collins witnessed the final time the great writer reached for a pen and put it to paper.

William Walker (1608–1680)

O, 'tis a parlous boy:
Bold, quick, ingenious, forward, capable.

Richard III, act 3, scene 1

Shakespeare had at least seven friends who christened one of their male children William. In London both John Heminges and Richard Burbage had sons named William (and John Heminges' William was also a playwright). In Stratford, Hamnet Sadler, Thomas Greene, Richard Tyler, and the mercer Henry Walker each had a son called William, while in Oxford, John Davenant named his fourth and youngest son William. Both Davanant and Walker asked Shakespeare to be godfather to their newborn Williams. The baptism of William Walker was on October 16, 1608, one of the few records that enable us to place Shakespeare in a given place at a given time. On that day he was in Trinity Church, Stratford, with his friend Henry Walker, high bailiff of Stratford, standing godfather to Walker's newborn son. When Shakespeare died, young William Walker was seven years old, close to the age of Shakespeare's granddaughter, Elizabeth Hall. Shakespeare left the little boy, his godson, twenty shillings in gold in his will. Death denied Shakespeare's own son, Hamnet, a future; but William Walker carried the poet's first name into the next generation and, in 1649, like Shakespeare's father John, and Walker's own father, Henry, William Walker became high bailiff of Stratford.

Shakespeare's London Friends

‡‡⇌ ⇌‡‡

In Which We See How Shakespeare's Life in London Differed from His Life in Stratford

> London is the only place in which the
> child grows completely up into the man.
> *Essays: On Londoners and Country People*, William Hazlitt

When Shakespeare arrived in London at the end of the 1580s, he found an atmosphere radically different from Stratford's. Even the entrance to the city was dramatic, for London was still a walled city. To approach it was to see the fortifications from a distance, and to enter it meant coming first through the suburban overflow of the fast-growing metropolis, then through one of the great stone gates.

With a population of over 100,000 people, London was the largest city in Europe. Built in an arch from the ominous Tower on the east side, to the city of Westminster on the west, the walls compressed the city along its northern border. On the south stretched the Thames River, teeming with small river taxis, boats that off-loaded exotic cargoes from the far-off corners of the world, and ships that circumnavigated the globe.

The city rang with the noise of horses and carriages negotiating the narrow streets, church bells tolling, street vendors hawking their wares, victims of cutpurses crying out, boatmen calling for passengers, and conversations buzzing. Pungent odors assailed the nose from the unwashed populace and from the sewage that ran in open gutters down to the river.

A palpable energy enlivened the city. A place of danger and excitement, London was the seat of government, the source of decision making, and the center of commerce, entertainment, and art. The powerful in London rewarded achievement and failure, doled out praise and exacted punishment, established who was in, who was out. From the Tower the groans of tortured prisoners could be heard. Heads of criminals and traitors were displayed on pikes on London Bridge. In 1587, shortly before Shakespeare's arrival, Mary Queen of Scots had been beheaded in the Tower. A few days later, a great funeral procession for Sir Philip Sidney wound its way through the London streets to his burial site in St. Paul's Cathedral. And in 1588 the formidable Spanish Armada—a huge naval convoy that threatened England with almost certain defeat and the prospect of Spanish invasion and Spanish rule—had been defeated. Into the mix of euphoria and optimism, suspicion and treachery, honor and idealism that filled London in the late 1500s, William Shakespeare came to write plays.

The Theatre, the first structure designed only for the performance of plays, had been built in 1576 by James Burbage. Soon after came the Curtain. They stood outside the walls just north of the city. In 1588 Philip Henslowe built a similar structure, the Rose, on the south bank of the Thames. These three theatres—built outside the city proper to avoid civic restrictions, yet close enough to draw the London audience— provided homes for the growth and flowering of the English renaissance theatre. They were Shakespeare's London destination.

Shakespeare's earliest friends connected him with his home in Stratford. Through Richard Field he was introduced to the publishing world in London. Now the new friends he made through his work in the London theatre would bring him into the chaotic world of play production, into the legal world of the Inns of Court, and into the glamorous world of the aristocrats who patronized writers and performers.

Friends of a Sort: Shakespeare and Royalty

To our English Terence Mr. William Shakespeare:
Some Say (good Will)—which I, in sport, do sing—

Hadst thou not played some kingly parts in sport,
Thou hadst been a companion for a king
And been a king among the meaner sort.
The Scourge of Folly (1610), John Davies of Hereford

One of the warmest patrons of the theatre at the end of the sixteenth century was Queen Elizabeth I. When James I became king in 1603 he exceeded her in his enthusiasm for plays, and for Shakespeare's company in particular. Though a friendship in the intimate sense could not have existed between a commoner playwright and his sovereign, with both Elizabeth and James, Shakespeare experienced the curious symbiotic relationship that exists between patron and artist.

Shakespeare's London was above all a political arena. The theatre interpreted the history of England and the issues of the day, and was scrutinized vigilantly by Queen Elizabeth's Master of the Revels.

Shakespeare's plays were censored and cut like any other pieces of writing: the deposition scene in *Richard II* was not allowed to be published, for instance, and all his plays had to be screened by the Master of the Revels before they could be performed. But as a writer Shakespeare seems not to have been hampered by censorship. The complex psychology of his characters interested Shakespeare more than polemical statements, so he set his political plays in historic periods (Greek and Roman), which removed the subject matter from too obvious a connection with present-day problems. Or he validated the current ruler by legitimizing Elizabeth's Tudor origins—the thrust of the history plays from *Richard II* through *Henry VI*—or James's Stuart background—the only reason for the apparition of all the former Scottish kings in *Macbeth*.

Shakespeare filled his plays with battle scenes, and included numerous condemnations to death. Treachery was punished. Severed heads were standard props, and Bardolph (*Henry V*) was hung for thievery on the battlefields of France.

Both Queen Elizabeth and King James were responsible for death and torture, and both struggled to escape blame for the horrific results of decisions they were forced to make. Queen Elizabeth's vacillation on signing the death warrant for Mary Queen of Scots is mirrored in Shakespeare's *Richard III* and *King John*, where the command to murder children is accomplished by implication and connivance rather than by a direct order.

The insight Shakespeare showed into the complex inner life of rulers, and the Byzantine maneuverings of those in power—or desiring power—must have made his plays especially appealing to both Elizabeth and James. Their own lives had been threatened in their youth by powerful, unscrupulous, and vicious factions. They survived by becoming cunning and devious. They both loved the theatre. And they both knew William Shakespeare.

Queen Elizabeth I (1533–1603)

She shall be, to the happiness of England
An aged princess; many days shall see her
And yet no day without a deed to crown it...
A most unspotted lily shall she pass
To the ground, and all the world shall mourn her.

Henry VIII, act 5, scene 5

Queen Elizabeth enjoyed a long and brilliant reign during which she was one of the greatest patrons known to the period of theatre that bears her name. Between 1590 (when Shakespeare was a new actor in London) and her death in 1603—thirteen years—Elizabeth commanded about ninety performances at her court. When Puritanism threatened entertainers, she protected the theatre companies against its sanctions.

A number of Court performances were routinely clustered around Christmastime. From 1591 to 1592, Lord Strange's Company performed six times from Christmas to early February, an unusual number of performances by a single troupe. But by then this company included the young Richard Burbage, plus Augustin Phillips, Thomas Pope, and William Sly, all names associated later with Shakespeare's in the Lord Chamberlain's Men. Was it this exceptional group of developing young actors that made Queen Elizabeth bring the Lord Chamberlain's company to court more than any other company? Or was it the plays of its rising young playwright, William Shakespeare?

Elizabeth had strong opinions about the plays performed for her. Legend has it that she so enjoyed Falstaff in court performances of *Henry IV, Parts 1* and *2* that she requested a play from Shakespeare that would show the old knight in love. Shakespeare is said to have complied by writing *The Merry Wives of Windsor* in just two weeks. What banter, what expressions of pleasure, what exchange of mutual respect must have occurred before and after these performances between the queen and the actors—behaviors expressing a friendship not able to flower among beings trapped in radically different levels of society.

John Harington, a scholar, translator, and courtier in Elizabeth's entourage observed: "when she smiles, it has a pure sunshine that everyone did choose to bask in if they could; but anon came a storm from a sudden gathering of clouds, and the thunder fell in wondrous manner on all."[1] Elizabeth's temper lashed out once at the Chamberlain's Men. Essex had been beheaded at the Queen's order in February 1601. Before his disastrous attempt at rebellion, his followers had paid for a performance of *Richard II* by the Chamberlain's Men, a performance that included the deposition scene so threatening to any sitting monarch. Challenging any possible admiration of Essex on the company's part and knowing Shakespeare's close relationship with Essex's follower Southampton, she insisted that the Chamberlain's Men perform for her the night before Essex's execution—a subtle and Machiavellian demonstration of her power.

In August of that year, the matter still haunted her. She said to her keeper of records, William Lambard, "I am Richard II, know ye not that?" And, in a seeming attack not only on Essex but on Shakespeare and his fellows, she continued: "He that will forget God will also forget his benefactors. This tragedy was played forty times in open streets and houses."[2] In spite of the company's perceived disloyalty, Elizabeth continued her patronage of the Chamberlain's Men.

But Shakespeare was his own man. During Queen Elizabeth's lifetime he resisted giving the fawning idolatry the queen received from other writers of the time. When Elizabeth died in 1603 Shakespeare wrote no encomiums. If the end of the queen's reign disillusioned him, he worked it out in writing *Hamlet* (1601–1602) and *Troilus and Cressida* (1603).

Respectful allusions to Elizabeth can be found in Shakespeare's early work, but they are most often metaphoric references, such as the line in Sonnet 107: "The mortal moon hath her eclipse endured." The moon in this case is interpreted to be Elizabeth, as is "a fair vestal throned by the west," referred to by Oberon in act 2, scene 1 of *A Midsummer Night's Dream*. The rare and guarded allusions to Elizabeth in Shakespeare's work indicate the need to acknowledge her, but not to be obsequious; to honor her, but not at the expense of his integrity—a subtle indication of an underlying and instinctive sense of his own equality and worth.

Near the end of his life, however, and long after Queen Elizabeth had died, Shakespeare looked back over the extraordinary time in which he had lived and ended his last play, *Henry VIII* (about Elizabeth's father), with this praise for the newborn Elizabeth and her heir James I:

>   Cranmer
>   Let me speak, sir,
> For heaven now bids me; and the words I utter
> Let none think flattery, for they'll find 'em truth.
> This royal infant—heaven still move about her!—
> Though in her cradle, yet now promises
> Upon this land a thousand blessings,
> Which time shall bring to ripeness. She shall be—
> But few now living can behold that goodness—
> A pattern to all princes living with her
> And all that shall succeed. Saba was never
> More covetous of wisdom and fair virtue
> Than this pure soul shall be. All princely graces
> That mould up such a mighty piece as this is
> With all the virtues that attend the good,
> Shall still be doubled on her. Truth shall nurse her,
> Holy and heavenly thoughts still counsel her;
> She shall be loved and feared. Her own shall bless her;
> Her foes shake like a field of beaten corn,
> And hang their heads with sorrow. Good grows with her;
> In her days every man shall eat in safety
> Under his own vine what he plants, and sing
> The merry songs of peace to all his neighbors.
> God shall be truly known, and those about her
> From her shall read the perfect ways of honour,
> And by those claim their greatness, not by blood.
> Nor shall this peace sleep with her; but as when
> The bird of wonder dies, the maiden phoenix,
> Her ashes new create another heir
> As great in admiration as herself
> So shall she leave her blessedness to one—
> When heaven shall call her from this cloud of darkness—
> Who from the sacred ashes of her honour
> Shall star-like rise, as great in fame as she was,
> And so stand fixed. Peace, plenty, love, truth, terror,
> That were the servants to this chosen infant,
> Shall than be his, and like a vine grow to him;

Wherever the bright sun of heaven shall shine
His honour and the greatness of his name
Shall be and make new nations; he shall flourish
And like a mountain cedar reach his branches
To all the plains about him; our children's children
Shall see this and bless heaven.
She shall be, to the happiness of England,
And aged princess; many days shall see her,
And yet no day without a deed to crown it.
Would I had known no more! But she must die—
She must, the saints must have her—yet a virgin,
A most unspotted lily shall she pass
To the ground, and all the world shall mourn her.

Unlike other Elizabethan playwrights and poets, Shakespeare wrote only for a company he co-owned. He provided plays he wished to write for actors who were his friends and colleagues, and he wrote his plays to please his own taste. But when Ben Jonson once described Shakespeare's poetry as the "flights...that did so take Eliza,"[3] he confirmed that the queen who loved the theatre knew and valued the greatest playwright of her age.

King James I (1566–1625)

Your children shall be kings
You shall be king.

Macbeth, act 1, scene 3

Elizabeth must have seemed an old lady to Shakespeare when he met her. By 1590 she was fifty-seven. Her successor, James I, the only son of Mary Queen of Scots and the man who first united Scotland and England in one kingdom, was two years Shakespeare's junior. He came to the throne in 1603 when Shakespeare was a successful London playwright, actor, and theatre owner thirty-nine years of age. One of James's first acts in office was to make the Chamberlain's Men the King's Men, claiming for himself the patronage of Shakespeare's company and thus acknowledging their brilliance.

At thirty-seven, James was physically unprepossessing, with legs so weak he had to lean on an attendant to walk and often had to be tied to the saddle when he rode (as he loved to do, often and recklessly). His tongue was too large for his mouth, giving his Scots speech a further impediment to English ears.

James I was born June 19, 1566. At just over a year old, he was proclaimed king of Scotland and installed at Stirling Castle for the first twelve years of his life. After infancy he never saw his mother and was cared for by the Earl and Countess of Mar. This honorable pair educated him and kept him safe. In later years James so trusted the Countess of Mar that he sought her out to care for his oldest son, the promising Prince Henry whose tragic death at eighteen destined his younger brother Charles to the throne.

James had a strong education in French and Latin. Despite the fervent Roman Catholicism that doomed his mother, and because of the strong Protestant faction in Scotland, James was brought up a Protestant and was well instructed in theology. Given that instruction, and his own intellectual and egocentric personality, he developed a pedantic streak. He loved to show off his writing and his learning. He also had a desire to preach. These personal qualities, combined with his sale of monopolies to unsavory favorites and his desire for an alliance with Spain, irritated his subjects.

James was called the "schoolmaster of the realm" by John Harington. But scholars surmise that his treatise on *Witchcraft in Scotland* contributed to the portrait of the witches in Shakespeare's *Macbeth*, which was written shortly after James's accession to the throne. James's most intriguing work to the modern reader might be the diatribe of 1604: *A Counterblast to Tobacco*.

James lacked the charisma that had enabled Elizabeth to enchant her public. His abrasive personality could offend both Puritans and Catholics, and his insistence on the doctrine of Divine Right crippled his relationship with Parliament. His blatant favoritism for handsome young men, and their influence over him, opened him to rumors, suspicion, and denigration.

What he shared with his great predecessor, however, was a determination to preserve the peace, and an extravagant love of plays. Now patron of the King's Men, James made Lawrence Fletcher, one of his favorite actors in Scotland, the first named actor of the company. Immediately following Fletcher's name was that of William Shakespeare. From 1603 on Shakespeare and his friends would be the King's Men, and one bit of evidence that shows the King's close relationship to them and his pride in the association was an order that they be paid over twenty pounds to be Grooms of the Chamber for a royal visit from the Spanish Constable of Castile.

James also patronized other theatre companies: The Queen's Men, Prince Henry's Men, Prince Charles's Men, and Lady Elizabeth's Men—every royal family member had a company of actors. And every year James saw approximately five times the number of plays Elizabeth had, over half presented by his own company, the King's Men. James was the real king, but if John Davies's poem represents the truth, Shakespeare often acted the king—and in writing and portraying kings, he held a mirror up to the king's nature.

Henry Wriothesley, the Earl of Southampton (1573–1624)

A woman's face with nature's own hand painted
Hast thou, the master mistress of my passion

Sonnet #20, William Shakespeare

So long as men can breathe or eyes can see
So long lives this, and this gives life to thee.

Sonnet #18, William Shakespeare

When Shakespeare left Stratford he was acquainted with members of the local gentry: his father made their highly decorated, elegant gloves and had commerce with them as an alderman and high bailiff. In addition, Shakespeare had a wide acquaintance of artisans, farmers, teachers, vicars, and small-businessmen in his native town. The bustling, fast-paced, diverse world of London, however, brought him a wider range of acquaintances.

The theatre was as public and as glamorous then as it is today. Young William Shakespeare not only appeared onstage with the best actors of the age, he was soon (with his *Henry VI* trilogy, c. 1591) writing some of London's most popular plays. These plays were seen by the entire range of Londoners, from apprentices, artisans, and laborers who spent their penny to stand in the yard, to the middle class and gentry sitting in the galleries, to the glittering aristocrats who often bought seats on the stage itself.

This last group was important to please. Theatre managers and companies needed patrons. Actors required the protection of a powerful aristocrat; they needed to become his actual servants, to receive his financial and legal support, in order to avoid being branded "rogues and vagabonds." By the Act of Vagabondage of 1572, without a company or a patron, an actor was considered a public nuisance vulnerable to almost arbitrary imprisonment or expulsion from the city.

Aristocrats sought out the excitement, creative energy, and glamour that pulsated around the live theatre. Actors swelled with pride at their applause. Aristocrats had money, power, and position; actors had an indefinable talent to move a crowd, a heightened imagination, and a fearless, thrilling, risk-taking freedom. Attraction and acquaintance between the two was common, as witness the relationship between the Lord and the Players in the Induction to *The Taming of the Shrew*, or Hamlet's easy, admiring comradeship with the Players in *Hamlet*. But close friendship, given the difference in rank, was rare and hard to sustain.

In 1593, not yet thirty years old, Shakespeare became friends with the extraordinary Earl of Southampton. Born in 1573, the Earl was a decade Shakespeare's junior. At barely twenty years old, he was acknowledged as a sparkling jewel of the aristocracy. Young, bright, and notoriously beautiful, he was sought out and adulated by men and women alike. Shakespeare might have seen him at the public theatre, at private performances, or the Inns of Court. He would have heard Southampton spoken of as both heir to vast estate holdings and the inheritor of his father's debts. Though beset with monetary problems, the young Earl of Southampton lived in as wealthy a style as his rank and title indicated he should; and he took such interest in the arts that many poets and writers appealed to him to be their patron.

From 1592 to 1594 all the theatres in London were closed to prevent the spread of the plague. Forced away from the theatre, Shakespeare tried his hand at serious—that is, respectable, literary, publishable—poetry, writing a long narrative poem on a classic subject: the love between Venus and Adonis. He dedicated it to the Earl of Southampton, requesting his patronage as follows:

> To the Right Honourable Henrie Wriothesley, Earl of Southampton, and Baron of Titchfield:
> Right Honourable, I know not how I shall offend in dedicating my unpolished lines to your Lordship, nor how the world will censure me for choosing so strong a prop to support so weak a burden. Only if your Honour seem but pleased, I account myself highly praised, and vow to

take advantage of all idle hours, till I have honoured you with some graver labour. But if the first heir of my invention prove deformed, I shall be sorry it had so noble a godfather, and never after ear so barren a land, for fear it yield me still so bad a harvest. I leave it to your honourable survey, and your Honour to your heart's content, which I wish may always answer your own wish, and the world's hopeful expectation.

Your Honour's in all duty,
William Shakespeare[4]

The poem must have pleased the earl, for Shakespeare set himself to "graver labour," and the following spring presented another epic poem. Its subject and title was *The Rape of Lucrece*. The dedication, again to the Earl of Southampton, reads:

The love I dedicate to your Lordship is without end; whereof this pamphlet, without beginning, is but a superfluous moiety. The warrant I have of your honourable disposition, not the worth of my untutored lines, makes it assured of acceptance. What I have done is yours; what I have to do is yours; being part in all I have, devoted yours. Were my worth greater, my duty would show greater; meantime, as it is, it is bound to your Lordship, to whom I wish long life still lengthened with all happiness.

Your Lordship's in all duty,
William Shakespeare[5]

The warmer and more personal tone of the second dedication argues a developing, close friendship between the poet and the twenty-year-old earl despite the differences in their background and status.

The Earl of Southampton's father had been a difficult man who quarreled violently with his wife, lived beyond his means, and was a rigorous Catholic in a Protestant country where popish sympathies often led to treasonous acts. He died when his son was just eight. Little Henry Wriothesley was placed as a ward with William Cecil, Lord Burghley, who, as Queen Elizabeth I's primary advisor, was one of the most powerful men in the realm. At twelve years old Southampton was sent to St. John's College, Cambridge, and at sixteen entered Gray's Inn.

Gray's Inn was one of the four London schools whose purpose was to teach the law to young aristocrats who were destined to administer large estates and help govern the country. Gray's Inn, Lincoln's Inn, and the Inner and Middle Temple had a society and culture all their own. Residences and colleges for high-spirited, bright, young aristocrats, their halls were often filled with banquets, festivities, games, and plays—plays that the young men wrote and acted in, as well as performances they hosted of plays by professional actors.

The first play written in blank verse was by Thomas Norton and Thomas Sackville, two aristocratic young men of the Inner Temple. It was called *Gorboduc* (1565). Its use of language was stiff compared to the blank verse plays that would follow from the hands of Marlowe and Shakespeare, but it was a milestone in the history of Elizabethan theatre, and was created at the Inns of Court. The students at the Inns of Court perpetuated the ideal of academic drama: they maintained that plays should adhere to classic patterns; that the unities of time, place, and action should be rigidly followed; and that only men of university education were capable of writing distinguished, admirable plays.

What must the encounter between the actors of Shakespeare's company and these young men have been like? A mutual respect, curiosity, and need bridged the distance between the budding aristocrats and the working artists, the wealthy estate owners and the masters of the acting craft.

Young people matured earlier four hundred years ago. Boys were routinely sent to Oxford and Cambridge at twelve or thirteen years of age. They went to the Inns of Court three or four years later, and by their early twenties were often in charge of important diplomatic missions. By the time Southampton reached eighteen, Burghley had begun a campaign to marry the earl to his granddaughter, Elizabeth Vere. Between 1591 and 1595 Southampton held out against this arranged marriage. At first he was simply more interested in his friends than in marriage. Then, in 1595, he came to know Elizabeth Vernon, the first cousin of the Earl of Essex, his great mentor. He fell so in love with her that when Ambrose Willoughby slandered her, Southampton actually tore out Willoughby's hair.

Despite incurring an enormous fine of five thousand pounds, which Burghley had the right to assess Southampton for the refusal to marry his granddaughter (and which came near to ruining the young man financially), the Earl of Southampton married Elizabeth Vernon in 1598. She was a maid of honor to the queen, and she was pregnant. She was also a first cousin of the Earl of Essex, who, when Southampton appeared to be reluctant, insisted he marry her. The ceremony was held in secret, and when it was discovered, Queen Elizabeth was infuriated: not only had Southampton flouted the wishes of Lord Burghley, her counselor, but the fornication committed was strictly forbidden among her ladies in waiting.

Despite his marriage, Southampton's androgynous beauty, the all-male surroundings of his college years, and his close friendship with unmarried men (the Danvers brothers) has caused speculation about his sexuality. Particularly at issue is the nature of his relationship with Shakespeare.

Southampton was young, beautiful, admired, and aristocratic, with somewhat feminine good looks. He had a volatile temperament and was quick to anger, but equally quick to charm. Exceedingly well educated and a lover of art and literature, Southampton must have seemed the incarnation of every glamorous vision or dream that had first brought Shakespeare to London.

The dedications of *Venus and Adonis* and *The Rape of Lucrece* to Henry Wriothesley, Earl of Southampton, are the only two documents that confirm a relationship between Shakespeare and the earl. Opinions on that relationship are speculative, but the historical research of A. L. Rowse, Robert Giroux, and others connect not only the great lyric poems of Shakespeare with Southampton, but identify Southampton convincingly as the recipient of the most self-revelatory body of writing in all Shakespeare's works: the *Sonnets*.

The man about whom we think we know so little reveals the depths of his emotional life in 154 short poems. If read in order, the sonnets give us a remarkable picture of Shakespeare in the early 1590s. If autobiographical, they reveal a tormented time in his life.

The first seventeen sonnets are directed to a young aristocrat who is resisting marriage; the speaker pleads with him to marry so as to leave a copy of himself and continue his family line. Shakespeare could well have written these poems as a result of being commissioned by—or in hopes of pleasing—either Burghley or Southampton's mother, both of whom were desperate for a marriage to center the young man. The need for Southampton to marry, and the descriptions of the beauty and gentility of the young man addressed in the first seventeen sonnets, urge the identity of one with the other.

Sonnet #18 ("Shall I compare thee to a summer's day?") suddenly reveals the attraction the young recipient has come to exert on the poet, while *Sonnet #20* confirms that this recipient is a beautiful, androgynous young man ("thou master/mistress of my passion"). The poet claims himself resigned not to act on his attraction as Nature has "pricked out" the beloved idol for women's pleasure.

The *Sonnets* then trace the agony of the poet in his separation from the young man, his eagerness for them to reunite, and his arguments with himself as to his feelings. His love is sorely tested when another poet presents himself and his work to Southampton for patronage. The only poet likely to threaten Shakespeare's confidence at the time was the young Christopher Marlowe, who was writing *Hero and Leander* as if in competition with Shakespeare's *Venus and Adonis*, and who also wanted Southampton for his patron. The rival poet's death, remarked upon in the *Sonnets*, further suggests his identity as Christopher Marlowe and thus confirms the date of the sonnets as the early 1590s (Marlowe died in 1593).

The final sonnets introduce the famous Dark Lady, a black-eyed, musical temptress loved by both the poet and his friend, whom the poet says he is willing to give up to the earl. The plays Shakespeare was writing in the early 1590s replay the agony and the ecstasy of the friendship revealed in the *Sonnets*. At the end of *Two Gentlemen of Verona*, two friends and rivals in love, Valentine and Proteus, are reconciled on the slimmest of pretexts. Out of frustrated, unrequited passion, Proteus threatens to force himself on Sylvia, the woman his friend Valentine loves. When caught and stopped by Valentine, Proteus's hasty apology produces instant forgiveness. So deep is the love between the two men and so happy are they to be reconciled that Valentine, as affirmation of the superiority of the love between men, offers to Proteus his part in Sylvia's love. Is this the acting out of classical philosophy? Or is it wishful thinking on Shakespeare's part?

The Merchant of Venice is often dated at about 1594, and its title character is an older man named Antonio who opens the play saying, "I know not why I am so sad." Though he denies being in love, as the play unfolds it would appear that Antonio's sadness is rooted in his love for Bassanio. The handsome young Bassanio wishes to marry an elegant and wealthy woman. Antonio helps to effect the marriage—at the potential cost of his own life. Several years later, another Antonio, young Sebastian's friend in *Twelfth Night*, is willing to make a similar sacrifice. Thus, the poignant, bittersweet character who is left out, the lonely presence to whom love is denied, who gives depth to the great Shakespearean comedies (Antonio in *The Merchant of Venice*; later, Don Pedro in *Much Ado About Nothing*; Jacques in *As You Like It*; Malvolio, Antonio, and Feste in *Twelfth Night*) makes his first appearance at this time.

Writing comes from experience and imagination, and is always self-revelatory. It requires making choices, and these choices (consciously or unconsciously triggered) cannot but reveal aspects of the author's personal life. However, if the thematic choices in the works of Shakespeare between 1592 and 1596 suggest a deep attraction between Shakespeare and the Earl of Southampton, their association seems to have been brought to an end by the latter year. Southampton rode off to join his admired Essex as a courtier and a soldier and begin his adult life.

Except for the year 1599, when Rowland Whyte reports that Southampton and his friend Rutland, stuck in town for a time, did "pass away the tyme in London merely going to plaies every Day," we have evidence of only two further connections between Shakespeare and the earl.[6] When Southampton took part in the disastrous Essex rebellion (1601) he was imprisoned and was fortunate (as Essex was not) to escape with his life. After Elizabeth died in 1603, James acceded to the throne and Southampton was released from prison. Shakespeare's feelings were expressed in *Sonnet #107*, which Robert Giroux argues was written in 1603, ten years after the other sonnets:

> Not mine own fears nor the prophetic soul
> Of the wide world dreaming on things to come
> Can yet the lease of my true love control,
> Supposed as forfeit to a confined doom.
> The mortal Moon hath her eclipse endured
> And the sad augurs mock their own presage.
> Uncertainties now crown themselves assured
> And peace proclaims olives of endless age.
> Now with the drops of this most balmy time
> My love looks fresh, and Death to me subscribes,
> Since spite of him I'll live in this poor rhyme,
> While he insults o'er dull and speechless tribes.
> And thou in this shall find thy monument,
> When tyrants crests and tombs of brass are spent.[7]

In his masterful analysis of the sonnets, *The Book Known as Q*, Robert Giroux notes all the contemporary references in this poem: Queen Elizabeth was often referred to as the Moon, and the eclipse in line six thus refers to her death. The references to tyrants in the last line refers to her tyrannical acts (a reference that would not have been permitted before her death), perhaps in particular her incarceration of Raleigh, Southampton, Essex, and others, and her execution of Essex. "Tombs of brass" refers to the great brass tomb near where her body lay shortly after death, awaiting the construction of a marble tomb that would take years to complete. "And peace proclaims olives of endless age" refers to the accession of James I to the throne, bringing relief from the uncertainty that surrounded Elizabeth's death and peace with Scotland, Ireland, and Spain. "My love looks fresh" carries with it the familiar Shakespearean double meaning: (1) his own feelings of love "look fresh" seeing the earl suddenly released from prison, and (2) the fact that when the earl was released he still looked young (he was in fact only twenty-nine). And finally, "the drops of this most balmy time" refer to the rejoiced-in warm, gentle rains of the spring of 1603, and (double meanings again) the tears of grief for the passing of Elizabeth and joy for the peaceful accession of James.

Most revealing is the first quatrain, indicating Shakespeare's fear—which seems to stem from an abiding love—of Southampton's imprisonment, a condition he was powerless to change. But the poet offered Southampton the unique gift he always promised: when all else was gone, what Shakespeare wrote of him would last.

Southampton's two years and four months in prison matured him; afterwards he became a model husband, father, and public servant. He would have seen Shakespeare's plays to the end of his life. On January 12 and 13, 1605, Shakespeare and Southampton encountered each other again, perhaps for the last time. Queen Anne was on a tour for the holiday season. She was invited to Southampton's estate of Titchfield and celebratory performances were needed. The call went out for entertainment ("players, jugglers, and such kind of creatures"[8]). Richard Burbage, responding for the King's Men to this request, said they had no new play ready, but could offer *Love's Labours Lost*, a light comedy whose "wit and mirth" he felt would please the queen. Was Burbage aware of the undercurrents in this choice of play and the possible irony in the title? Did Shakespeare himself suggest it?

Love's Labours Lost was written in the early 1590s, the same time as the *Sonnets*, the time Wilson suggests Shakespeare was in residence with the Earl of Southampton. The play's title came from a book by John (Giovanni) Florio, a linguist and tutor to the earl. The story, one of Shakespeare's few predominantly original story ideas, concerns four young noblemen. One of them, the king of Navarre, in his glamour, intelligence, and nobility, reminds the reader of the young Southampton. This king has determined that he and his three friends should establish an academy, and for three years forego any relationship with women in favor of the pursuit of knowledge. A visit from the princess of France compels Navarre, out of respect and diplomacy, to temporarily put aside his plans for the celibate academy. The complications of the play evolve as each of the young men falls in love with the princess and her gentlewomen, and as they find each other out. The ending is melancholic and autumnal, however. The king of France has died and the princess must return home in mourning. The young men and women separate, each promising to wait a year before renewing their relationship, and the play ends with one of Shakespeare's most perfect, bittersweet songs.

What must it have felt like to Shakespeare to re-explore this play ten years after its creation? Did it seem a valedictory to Southampton and the extraordinary days of their youth?

Shakespeare left no memento for Southampton in his will, wrote no further narrative poems or sonnets, dedicated no further works to him. The Earl of Southampton took his place wandering through the poet's mind and imagination, consistently in Shakespeare's view through his public life, but no longer one of Shakespeare's close friends.

Emilia Bassano Lanier (1569–1645)

My mistress' eyes are nothing like the sun,
Coral is far more red than her lips red,
If snow be white, why then her breasts are dun
If hairs be wires, black wires grow on her head
Sonnet #130, William Shakespeare

Emilia Lanier, one of the best female poets of Shakespeare's age, is also the leading candidate to be identified as Shakespeare's unnamed Dark Lady of the sonnets. She was born Emilia Bassano, the eldest daughter of Baptiste Bassano and his reputed wife Margaret Johnson. Her father was a member of the extended Bassano family who had arrived from Venice to become court musicians at the time of Henry VIII. When Emilia was six her father died, and by the time she was seventeen she had also lost her mother.

She had been raised in the household of the Duchess of Kent perhaps as a waiting maid or musician. She became the mistress of Henry Carey, a man forty-five years her senior, who was both Lord Hunsdon and Queen Elizabeth's Lord Chamberlain, later the patron of Shakespeare's acting company. When Carey discovered Emilia was pregnant in 1592, he married her off to Alfonso Lanier, another musician—one of the fifty-nine who played at Queen Elizabeth's funeral. Emilia was trapped in this unhappy marriage when, according to A. L. Rowse, she became involved in a triangular relationship with Shakespeare and the Earl of Southampton.

Lord Hunsdon had a history of sponsoring acting companies dating back to 1564, so Shakespeare and his friends might have seen him accompanied by his young mistress when the company performed for the aristocracy. After their marriage Lanier and perhaps Emilia would have performed at court functions. We know that an acquaintance developed with Southampton, for the earl later recommended that Lanier receive the right to collect money for the weighing of hay and straw in London to augment his income. The stage was set for Shakespeare and Southampton to encounter the tantalizing Emilia in and around the court.

The Lady is described in the sonnets as dark complected with black hair and eyes—predictable coloring for a woman with an Italian background. She is well known, temperamental, proud, demanding, capricious—and a fine musician. *Sonnet #150* claims that pity for her situation first attracted Shakespeare to her:

> If thy unworthiness raised love in me,
> More worthy I to be beloved of thee.

And *Sonnet #128* describes her playing the virginals (an early, harpsichord-type instrument). In this sonnet Shakespeare calls her "my music." Their relationship was tempestuous and agonizing for Shakespeare, for the handsome, aristocratic young Southampton was the lady's real interest.

A great deal of fascinating information about Emilia Lanier comes from the diaries of Simon Forman (discovered in Oxford's Bodleian Library and analyzed by A. L. Rowse). Forman was a doctor and astrologer often consulted by upper-class women such as Maria Mountjoy and ladies of the court. As he needed personal details to cast horoscopes, his notes on his patients are unusually intimate and informative. Emilia visited him repeatedly and they began a sexual relationship as tormenting for him as her relationship with Shakespeare was for the poet.

Shakespeare seems to have recovered from his infatuation for Emilia, though Agatha Christie wrote a letter to the *London Times* wherein she attributes the character of Cleopatra, written a dozen or more years after Shakespeare's affair, to Shakespeare's memory of Emilia Lanier.[9]

After a conversion experience, Emilia wrote a long religious poem, *Salve Deus Rex Judaeorum*, accompanied by ten florid dedicatory poems addressed to various aristocratic women. These include the Countesses of Pembroke, Kent, Bedford, and Cumberland as well as Queen Anne herself. One dedication is "To all Vertuous Ladies in Generall."[10] As a body, the poems constitute a surprisingly strong feminist statement, including a defense of Eve that blames Adam for eating the apple. According to Rowse, Emilia's passionate prose introduction, filled with feminist ideas, is unlike anything else in Elizabethan and Jacobean literature.[11] The Shakespeare *Sonnets*, which present a jarringly unflattering picture of the Dark Lady, had just been published (without Shakespeare's permission) in 1609. Emilia's poems, published in 1611 and strongly defending women, can be read as her riposte to this slanderous characterization.

Throughout her poems Emilia Lanier shows how educated she is by continually making references to classical and biblical personages. But the last of her poems was a lyrical *Description of Cooke-ham* (Cookham), where she had spent time in her youth with the Duchess of Cumberland and her daughter Anne Clifford.

> The Trees with leaves, with fruits, with flowers clad,
> Embraced each other, seeming to be glad,
> Turning themselves to beauteous Canopies,
> To shade the bright Sunne from your brighter eies:
> The cristall Streames with silver spangles graced,
> While by the glorious Sunne they were embraced:
> The little Birds in chirping notes did sing,
> To entertaine both You and that sweet Spring. . . .
> Oh how me thought each plant, each floure, each tree
> Set forth their beauties then to welcome thee:
> The very Hills right humbly did descend,
> When you to tread upon them did intend.[12]

Emilia Lanier died in 1645, outliving most of Shakespeare's other contemporaries. The last half of her life was beset with financial problems. She had to teach the children of aristocrats in order to earn money, and she brought a lawsuit against her landlord in a rental dispute that was filled with "rude speeches" from both parties. The outcome was an unsuccessful eviction notice, followed by her abandonment of the apartment, which she left in "a nasty and filthy state."

Her son by Henry Carey, also called Henry, was a flautist for the king and gave Emilia two grandchildren, Mary and Henry. Her son died in 1633. Emilia then petitioned to regain the money for weighing hay and straw that was granted to her husband as a result of Southampton's recommendation. She had given the grant to her brother-in-law in exchange for a guarantee of half the profits, but he failed to pay her. She then claimed she had two grandchildren to support, and after a number of petitions, was granted what seemed to her an unsatisfactory amount of ten pounds a year plus arrears.

Despite its many flattering dedicatory poems, her book seems not to have sold. Only four copies are now known to exist. However, Emilia Lanier's *Salve Deus Rex Judaeorum* and Shakespeare's *Sonnets* remain two of the most revelatory documents concerning the elusive Shakespeare's life and times. And the printings were so restricted, the distribution so slight, it seems miraculous they each survived.

The Earls and the Countess of Pembroke

Henry Herbert, 2nd Earl of Pembroke c. 1534–1601
Mary Sidney Herbert, Countess of Pembroke c. 1561–1621
Sir Philip Sidney 1554–1586
William Herbert, 3rd Earl of Pembroke 1580–1630
Philip Herbert, 4th Earl of Pembroke 1584–1650

The Actors are come hither, my lord...
The best actors in the world.

Hamlet, act 2, scene 2

The story of Shakespeare and the Earl of Pembroke is one of a friendship with a family, and it dates back to Shakespeare's early days in London when he was an actor moving in and out of various companies. One of these companies had been founded by Henry Herbert, second Earl of Pembroke. In existence from 1592 to 1600, Pembroke's Men performed the three parts of Shakespeare's *Henry VI* and *Titus Andronicus*, which suggests that Shakespeare wrote for them and likely acted with them at least briefly.

As Pembroke's Men had to tour during the plague of 1593–1594, the question of Shakespeare's whereabouts at that time is interesting: Was he with the Earl of Southampton at Titchfield writing *Venus and Adonis* (as Ian Wilson argues in *Shakespeare, The Evidence*), or did he write the poem while touring as part of Pembroke's company? Regardless, he became acquainted with Pembroke at this time and benefited from his patronage as the company produced his earliest work.

The tangled world of Elizabethan acting companies becomes part of Shakespeare's story here, however, because Lord Strange's (pronounced like "sang") Men, an older company that disbanded in 1594, also produced the *Henry VI* trilogy and *Titus*. Shakespeare's destiny was shaping itself with these associations, for members of Lord Strange's Men (also known briefly as Derby's Men since Lord Strange became Earl of Derby in 1593) included Richard Burbage, George Bryan, Augustin Phillips, Thomas Pope, and William Sly, all of whom later became members of the Chamberlain's Men, the first Globe Theatre company.

Complicating the picture is the Queen's Men, Queen Elizabeth's own company, and its great rival, the Admiral's Men. The Queen's Men was founded in 1583, and as the queen could recruit any actors she wanted, the company was from its beginning the most important acting company in London. On June 13, 1587, the group was on a summer tour and was playing near Stratford in Thame, Oxfordshire, when a disaster occurred. An actor, William Knell (who played such distinguished roles as Prince Hal in an early non-Shakespearean version of *Henry V*) assaulted a colleague and was stabbed in the neck and killed in the subsequent fight. In September the company played Stratford and speculation arose that Shakespeare might have been hired to replace William Knell. This would take Shakespeare to London for the winter season of 1587 with the Queen's Men, where the company played at James Burbage's Theatre, thus acquainting Shakespeare with the Burbage family who were to be so important in his career. The experience also introduced him at court, where he would begin to encounter aristocrats like the Pembrokes who patronized various theatre companies.

The great comic Richard Tarlton was also a key member of the Queen's Men and the fortunes of the company started to decline after his death in 1588. Once in London, however, Shakespeare could float from company to company as did so many other actors at this time. In 1590 and 1591 he was probably a member of the combined Admiral's Men and Lord Strange's Men, for the printed texts of *Henry VI, Parts 2* and *3* identified John Holland and John Sincklo as actors in those plays, and they were known to belong to these companies. The Admiral's Men and Lord Strange's Men played at James Burbage's

Theatre (as had the Queen's Men) and at the head of the company was the greatest Marlovian actor of the end of the century, Edward Alleyn. In 1591 Alleyn quarreled with Burbage, and Alleyn took a group of his followers to Philip Henslowe's Rose Theatre, across the river in Southwark. The plague of 1593–1594 inspired the companies to combine again for a provincial tour (Was Shakespeare with them? Or with Pembroke's Men? Or with Southampton at Titchfield?), but they separated again upon their return to London in 1594. The Admiral's Men with Alleyn and the plays of Christopher Marlowe went to Henslowe at the Rose for the next six years, and Lord Strange's Men became the Lord Chamberlain's Men with Richard Burbage as the leading actor and, by December 1594, with William Shakespeare both acting and writing plays.

In fact, Shakespeare's partnership in the Chamberlain's Men relates him back to Southampton, as legend has it that Southampton re-warded Shakespeare's labors on his two great poems with a gift of a thousand pounds, an amount so huge as to encourage disbelief. However, there is proof that Shakespeare had access to a major amount of money at this time, for he was suddenly able to buy into the Chamberlain's Men as a shareholder. In any event, from 1596 on these two great companies vied with each other in acting talent and repertory, the Admiral's men producing plays by George Chapman, Thomas Dekker, Michael Drayton, Thomas Heywood and Anthony Munday, among others; the Chamberlain's Men boasting the talents of Shake-speare and, beginning in 1598, of Ben Jonson.

Pembroke's Men meanwhile played for Queen Elizabeth at court in 1592, and at the start of the plague in 1593 they toured. However, by the fall of that year, Philip Henslowe's diary shows that they were forced to sell their costumes to pay their debts. They also let other people publish some of the plays in their repertory, indicating their financial need to sell the rights to these plays. From 1595 to 1596 a revived Pembroke's Men's company set off on another tour, and in 1597 they played a London season at the Swan. They were unhappy in their choice of opening play, however: Thomas Nashe's *Isle of Dogs* was thought to be seditious in its satire. Making matters worse, three of the play's actors (Gabriel Spencer, Ben Jonson, and Robert Shaw) were imprisoned, and as it was July and theatres were closing for the summer, they shut down until October (by which time several of the actors had left the company to join the Admiral's Men). In 1595 a bad quarto of *Henry VI, Part 3* indicates that this play was in Pembroke's repertory, as was *Titus Andronicus* and an early version (not likely

Shakespeare's) of a play called *The Taming of a Shrew*, plus works by Christopher Marlowe and Thomas Kyd, among others.

By 1600 Lord Pembroke's company had two failed productions at Philip Henslowe's Rose theatre, which marked the end of Pembroke's company. It did not, however, mark the end of Shakespeare's connection with the family. Like the intricate braiding of boxwood hedges in an Elizabethan knot garden, Shakespeare's London relationships started to weave together in interconnecting patterns.

Lord Pembroke's company probably failed because he took little interest in it. Politics was his great interest and Shakespeare was forming acquaintance with a family whose national and international political and artistic connections went far beyond the local political activities of John Shakespeare. Around the Pembrokes Shakespeare was in heady company.

The second Earl of Pembroke's aunt was Queen Catherine Parr, the last of Henry VIII's six wives. Pembroke's first wife was Lady Jane Grey's sister and the marriage was dissolved in the reign of Queen Mary. After his second wife (the daughter of the Earl of Shrewsbury) died, Pembroke married Mary Sidney. This was in 1577, when he was thirty-nine and his young wife only sixteen. He was involved with the trial of Mary Queen of Scots, and in 1586 became president of the Council of Wales. In 1588 (the Armada year), he raised an army in Wales at his own cost and did it again in 1599. His health was failing at this time, however, and he died in 1601. His devotion to Wales is suggested to have been a stimulus to Shakespeare's creation of the Welsh characters in his plays.

Lady Pembroke, his third wife, was three years older than Shakespeare and was one of the remarkable women of the age. When Shakespeare created characters such as Rosalind or Viola or Imogen, surely Mary Herbert, Countess of Pembroke, came to mind as an assurance that such women existed. Her brother was the great poet Sir Philip Sidney, and her uncle the Earl of Leicester. Poets found in her a generous patron, and Edmund Spenser wrote one of the dedicatory sonnets of *The Faerie Queene* to her.

Her brother, Sir Philip Sidney, wrote *Arcadia* for her amusement, and the affection between them leaps across the years in his dedication:

> To my dear lady and sister the Countess of Pembroke. . . . Read it then at
> your idle times, and the follies your good judgment will find in it, blame
> not, but laugh at. And so, looking for no better stuff than, as in a
> haberdasher's shop, glasses or feathers, you will continue to love the

writer who doth exceedingly love you, and most most heartily prays you may long live to be a principal ornament to the family of the Sidneys.

Your loving brother, Philip Sidney[13]

When Sidney died of gangrene in the leg following a wound received in the wars in the Netherlands, the grieving countess supervised the completion of his work. An author and translator in her own right, she translated the Psalms, and then, as she found English theatre barbarous, she translated (in hopes of introducing them to English audiences) the "correctly written" plays of French dramatist Robert Garnier. When Queen Elizabeth planned to come to Wilton, the Pembroke estate, Mary wrote a dialogue called *Astraea* to entertain her. Poets whom Mary housed, inspired, and encouraged included Samuel Daniel, Edmund Spenser, William Brown, and Nicholas Breton, and her library contained so many books that Wilton was likened to a college.

A nineteenth-century tradition traceable to a tutor named William Cory (who came to Wilton from Eton in 1865) insists there was a letter from Mary Herbert to her son William, asking him to invite King James and Queen Anne to Wilton as "we have the man Shakespeare with us."[14] The letter has never been found, but the King's Men did present a performance at Wilton in October 1603. Shortly after King James arrived in London, in the middle of coronation festivities, the plague crept into London. By the end of the summer the theatres were all closed and London was deserted. King James and his court were staying with the Pembrokes and as the King's Men were at Mortlake in Surrey on tour, they were called to perform at Wilton. A belief persists that the production offered was *As You Like It*.

Mary Sidney Herbert had two sons, each of whom in succession became the Earl of Pembroke. The first, William Herbert, third Earl of Pembroke, lived from 1580 to 1630. Because of his initials he is a candidate for the W. H. to whom the sonnets of Shakespeare were dedicated (by the publisher). He is too young to make this claim tenable, however. A would-be poet, his most public youthful indiscretion was with Mary Fitton, one of Queen Elizabeth's ladies-in-waiting, whom he impregnated and then refused to marry. Those who claim Pembroke might have been the desirable young man in the *Sonnets* find Mary Fitton a likely candidate for the Dark Lady, though once again the dates do not easily mesh. Pembroke was confined to Fleet Street prison for his dalliance, then sent abroad. Several years later he married the

Earl of Shrewsbury's daughter and, like the Earl of Southampton, settled into productive civil service, ultimately becoming chancellor of Oxford University, where Pembroke College bears his name to this day.

Pembroke was a great friend and supporter of Ben Jonson, generously giving him twenty pounds a year with which to buy books. He developed a special fondness for Shakespeare's friend, the actor Richard Burbage. On May 20, 1619, shortly after Burbage died, Pembroke wrote to a friend, Lord Doncaster, that he could not bear to go see the play that night because "being tender-hearted (I) could not endure (to see it) so soon after the loss of my old friend Burbage."[15]

Pembroke was Lord Chamberlain and was responsible for vetting play scripts for publication from 1615–1626. His most permanent relationship to Shakespeare is found in the opening pages of the First Folio, for Shakespeare's friends John Heminges and Henry Condell dedicated the collection of Shakespeare's plays to the earl and his brother, the Earl of Montgomery.

It was surely an honor for Shakespeare to have had this lengthy connection with the family of the Earls of Pembroke. Four centuries later it must be an even greater source of pride to the Pembroke family that they can claim their ancestors were friends of William Shakespeare.

Lady Warwick (?–1603)

Here comes fair Mistress Anne.
The Merry Wives of Windsor, act 1, scene 1

For forty years Anne Russell, Countess of Warwick, was lady-in-waiting to Queen Elizabeth. She was with the queen when she died and followed her in death shortly thereafter. Her niece, Anne Clifford, daughter of Lady Warwick's beloved sister and constant companion Lady Cumberland, kept a diary that gives us a young, personal, and feminine witness to Elizabeth's final months, and to James's accession to the throne.

Anne Russell, the daughter of Francis, Earl of Bedford, was the Earl of Warwick's third wife. He was the older brother of the queen's favorite, the Earl of Leiscester. Warwick married Anne Russell in 1565 when he was thirty-seven, a marriage arranged by Leiscester, and evidently approved by the queen as it was held in the Chapel Royal and accompanied with great festivity.

Like the Earl of Pembroke, for a number of years the Earl of Warwick sponsored a company of actors. From 1574 to 1575 Warwick's men appeared in Stratford at the height of John Shakespeare's status and influence there, so at the age of ten William Shakespeare likely saw their performances, or certainly was aware of their appearance.

Decades later Lady Warwick would have known Shakespeare from his many appearances in plays at court, and as Warwickshire residents they would have taken that natural interest in each other of people who come from the same small corner of the world. Shakespeare would have known her as the Lady of the Manor of Rowington in his own home shire and recognized her and her sister as two of the distinguished ladies of the court, a group Violet Wilson calls "the truest, wisest, greatest era of womanhood"—women who were patterns for Rosalind and Viola and Portia.[16]

But a business dealing brought Lady Warwick and Shakespeare into closer proximity than the theatre and the court. In 1602, the year after his father's death, Shakespeare added to his property in Stratford by purchasing a cottage and a quarter acre of land in Chapel Lane facing his own New Place garden. The property belonged to the Rowington estate (the copyhold of one of the other small pieces of property belonging to this estate was for a time held by Shakespeare's friend Hamnet Sadler) and Violet Wilson claims in her *Society Women of Shakespeare's Time* that as a result of Shakespeare "failing to comply with some formalities due to Lady Warwick as lady of the manor, the property remained in her hands till Shakespeare made a special journey into Warwickshire to rectify his error, and obtained the copyhold from her ladyship."[17] Once more, through his contact with Lady Warwick, Shakespeare is revealed to be equally at home in the world of the theatre and the world of property, the world of art and the world of business, surrounded on the one hand by actors and writers, and on the other by lawyers and aristocrats.

As a last footnote, Anne Clifford, Lady Warwick's diarist/niece, was trapped for years in a miserable marriage to Richard Sackville, the Earl of Dorset, who turned out to be a compulsive gambler. She had two daughters to care for and after Dorset's death in 1624, being left heavily in debt, she swore she would never remarry. However, in 1630 she was persuaded to change her mind by none other than Philip Herbert, one of the brothers to whom Shakespeare's First Folio was dedicated. As Philip Herbert later became the Earl of Pembroke, the marriage united two brilliant households notable for their appreciation and support of William Shakespeare.

Maria Mountjoy (?–1606)

Haply a woman's voice may do some good
When articles too nicely urged be stood on.

Henry V, act 5, scene 2

For several of his years in London, Shakespeare lived at the corner of Silver Street and Monkwell in the parish of St. Olave in the home of Christopher and Maria Mountjoy. It is possible he met the Mountjoys through Richard Field, who lived nearby, for like Richard Field's wife Jacqueline, the Mountjoys were immigrant French Huguenots. However it was not until 1602, about fourteen years after coming to London and eight years after publishing *The Rape of Lucrece* with one of Field's rival publishers, that Shakespeare moved into the lodgings he rented from the Mountjoys. Until then he had lived in a number of different places.

In 1593 he was paying his taxes in St. Helen's parish on the east side of town. Living on Bishopsgate Street, he was on the road to the Curtain and the Theatre, giving him easy access to the acting companies there. By 1597 he had moved to the Liberty of the Clink in Southwark which was across the river close to the site of the Bear Garden, the Rose Theatre, and the Globe which would open in 1599. This put him outside the city of London proper, south of the river where entertainment venues were free of the attempts of the city to control or close them. Marchette Chute paints a lively picture of life in the Clink, describing streets interlaced with ditches, and a subculture of boatmen busily ferrying play-goers and fans of bearbaiting and cockfighting back and forth across the river to the call of "Eastward, ho!" and "Westward, ho!"

About 1602 Shakespeare left the Liberty of the Clink, moved back across the river, into rented quarters with the Mountjoys, whose business was the making of extravagant decorations for the head called "tires." More than hats, these decorations were often exquisitely bejeweled, made of elaborate twistings of gold and silver wire, and cost (in today's values) hundreds of pounds. The Mountjoys were so skilled at this craft that they kept several apprentices and had made at least one "tire" for Queen Elizabeth. As the name Silver Street might indicate, this was a neighborhood of goldsmiths and silversmiths; there were several Halls of Guilds nearby, and it was also the neighboring parish to Aldermanbury, where Shakespeare's close friends Heminges and Condell lived.

At the Mountjoys, Shakespeare was close to Paternoster Row and the bookstores, near the Mermaid Tavern, and not far from the Blackfriars Theatre. In 1602 the theatre was owned by the Burbages but was restricted to presenting plays performed by the boy singer/actors of St. Paul's (though his friend Ben Jonson wrote for the boys' company, Shakespeare never did). James Burbage had hoped to use the space as an indoor theatre for his company, but the neighborhood was an elegant one and residents petitioned to keep out professional theatre performances. Richard Field was one of the residents who signed the petition and one wonders if this had a negative effect on his friendship with Shakespeare.

Shakespeare's eventual residence with the Mountjoys gives us one of the most personal glimpses into his domestic life thanks to a scandal within the family and a lawsuit requiring Shakespeare's testimony.

It appears Christopher and Maria Mountjoy did not have an idyllic marriage. During 1604, while Shakespeare was living with them, Maria was having an affair with Henry Wood, a nearby cloth dealer. Afraid she might be pregnant, Maria sought the advice of an astrologer/physician, Simon Forman, as to the possible pregnancy and also (curiously) as to whether she should leave her husband and set herself up in business with Mrs. Wood. The pregnancy turned out to be a false alarm and she decided against the business with Wood's wife. At home in the meantime, Maria's only daughter Mary was of marriageable age, and there were three eligible apprentices, one of whom was Stephen Belott. Belott had finished his apprenticeship and had just returned from a trip to Spain. As he was, according to report, a fine, upstanding young man ("a very good and industrious servant" were the words Shakespeare swore to), the Mountjoys were eager for him to wed Mary.[18] They asked their lodger, William Shakespeare, to help persuade Belott, which Shakespeare did.

The Belotts, once married, moved out of the parental household and set up business for themselves in competition with the Mountjoys. After Mrs. Mountjoy died (1606) they moved back in to help Maria's widower father, and joined their business to his. Christopher Mountjoy, however, had promised Stephen Belott sixty pounds dowry upon his marriage to Mary, and 200 pounds following his own death. Though Mrs. Mountjoy had begged her husband to be generous, he only gave Belott ten pounds and some household items. The combined household was unhappy, and ultimately the Belotts moved out again.

Finally, in 1612, after eight years of frustration, Belott feared that he and Mary were to be cut off altogether, and so he brought suit against Mountjoy for the money promised. As Shakespeare had acted as matchmaker between the two young people and might be supposed to have some knowledge of the monetary settlements, he was called from Stratford to testify. It is the record of this court case that has preserved so much information about this domestic incident. Shakespeare testified, however, that he had no memory of the particulars and refused to confirm the monetary amounts at issue, or what household goods were given to the couple.

This lack of support must have disappointed the Belotts. However, many others were brought to testify: a servant in the household, Joan Johnson, who remembered and testified to Shakespeare's part in the matchmaking; Daniell Nichols (a friend of the family), and William Eaton, one of the apprentices; and Nowell Mountjoy, Christopher Mountjoy's brother. None claimed to remember the financial arrangements and the suit was referred to elders of the French church for arbitration. From them we learn that both Christopher Mountjoy and Stephen Belott were considered to be *"desbauchez"* (debauched) and led a life *"desreglée"* (unregulated) and *"desbordée"* (undisciplined). They determined Mountjoy should pay Belott just a fraction of his claim (a little over six pounds), which a year later he still had not done. Life with his own family in Stratford must have seemed well regulated to William Shakespeare, compared to the degeneracy of life in Silver Street after the death of his friend Maria Mountjoy.

William Johnson (fl. 1591–1616)

What things have we seen
Done at the Mermaid! heard words that have been
So nimble, and so full of subtle flame,
As if that every one (from whence they came)
Had meant to put his whole wit in a jest,

And had resolved to live a fool the rest
˙ Of his dull life.

Letter to Ben Jonson from Master Francis Beaumont

In the early 1600s there was an inveterate traveler, wit, and letter-writer named Thomas Coryat. Following a walking trip across Europe, he wrote a memoir of this adventure called *Coryats Crudities* in which (among many other adventures) he tells how in Venice he "saw a woman act, a thing I never saw before . . . and they performed it with as good a grace . . . as every I saw in any masculine actor."[19] For this memoir he solicited introductory poems from his distinguished acquaintance. Those who wrote for him included Inigo Jones, John Donne, and Michael Drayton. Between October 1612 and his death in 1617, Coryat traveled to the Middle East, Afghanistan, Constantinople, and India. From these exotic destinations he wrote letters home to "The High Seneschal of the Right Worshipful Fraternity of Sirenaical Gentleman," a group that met weekly at the Mermaid Tavern.[20]

This group was the Friday Street Club, founded by Sir Walter Raleigh, and the members of the fraternity were John Donne, Ben Jonson, Inigo Jones, Francis Beaumont, and John Fletcher. The Mermaid Tavern, on the corner of Bread and Friday Streets, was an easy walk from Shakespeare's home on Silver Street and the proprietor was William Johnson. He was a friend of Shakespeare as, on March 10, 1613, Johnson was listed as a trustee with Shakespeare in the purchase of a house in Blackfriars.

Shakespeare, a shrewd businessman, would not have entered into a business deal with a man unless he liked and trusted him, so we can suppose William Johnson, the tavern owner, a valued acquaintance. We know Ben Jonson was an intimate friend of Shakespeare and Beaumont and Fletcher were his close colleagues. In all likelihood Shakespeare spent convivial time in the Mermaid Tavern, and yet he is not included in the list of names of those friends who belonged to the "fraternity" that met every Friday. According to John Aubrey, whose information came from William Beeston (son of Christopher Beeston, who acted with Shakespeare in Jonson's *Everyman in his Humour* [1598]), Shakespeare "was not a company keeper, lived in Shoreditch, would not be debauched, and, if invited to, wrote: he was in pain."[21] Perhaps this indicates that as important as friendship was to Shakespeare, he stood away from organized groups, preferring encounters with his friends to occur at work, spontaneously, or one-on-one. Or perhaps he just needed the time to write.

In 1613, after his retirement to Stratford, Shakespeare decided to buy the Blackfriars Gatehouse. This was a second-floor dwelling that straddled the entrance to the district. The cost was 140 pounds, more than double the cost of New Place in Stratford. Shakespeare put up the money, but he asked William Johnson of the Mermaid, John Jackson (about whom little is known other than that he was a shipping magnate from Hull and an habitue of the Mermaid), and John Heminges to be co-purchasers with him, perhaps wanting London residents to look after the property while he was in Stratford. Or perhaps he was concerned about inheritance: according to Marchette Chute, purchasing the house with trustees meant that Shakespeare's wife could not inherit, according to London law, the normal one-third of his property. Instead, the trustees would hand it over to two Stratford trustees, John Greene and Matthew Morris, who would hold it entailed for Shakespeare's daughter Susanna.

The building had a long history of harboring, hiding, and facilitating the escape of Catholics, and was filled with secret nooks and passages. It was even connected with the Gunpowder Plot as people were accused of plotting in one of the sitting rooms. Close to the Blackfriars Theatre, near the ferry crossing to the Globe, and not far from the homes of Heminges and Condell, it was the only piece of residential property Shakespeare ever owned in London. Perhaps this indicates that although Shakespeare had moved to Stratford, the draw of London and his friends there made him long for a residence that would enable him to visit often and frequently the city that had nurtured his professional life.

Michael Drayton (1563–1631)

Since there's no help, come let us kiss and part—
Nay, I have done, you get no more of me;
And I am glad, yea, glad with all my heart,
That thus so cleanly I myself can free.
Shake hands for ever, cancel all our vows,
And when we meet at any time again,
Be it not seen in either of our brows
That we one jot of former love retain.
Now at the last gasp of Love's latest breath,

When, his pulse failing, Passion speechless lies,
When Faith is kneeling by his bed of death,
And Innocence is closing up his eyes,
Now if thou wouldst, when all have given him over
From death to life thou might'st him yet recover.

The Parting, Michael Drayton

The establishment of a friendship between William Shakespeare and Michael Drayton rests on a tangential fact, an unsubstantiated anecdote that refuses to die, and the logic of likelihood.

The tangential fact is that Michael Drayton was a patient of Shakespeare's son-in-law, the physician Dr. John Hall. Dr. Hall records that he cured Michael Drayton, poeta laureatus, of a fever by treating him with "syrup of violets" at Clifford Chambers (a village just two miles south of Stratford).

The anecdote (from churchman John Ward, 1662) reports that shortly before Shakespeare's death, Ben Jonson and the abstemious Michael Drayton met with Shakespeare in Stratford, and, after drinking too much, Shakespeare took ill of a fever and died. The vitality of this get-together is suggested by Oliver Elton, who says of Jonson and Drayton, "Energy, hatred of sham, a tendency to shout too loud, some lack of the finer vision, a manly, almost heroic, acceptance of life; these qualities were common to both men."[22]

The logic of likelihood rests on the numerous parallels between Michael Drayton's life and Shakespeare's. The first is that they were both Warwickshire lads. Drayton was born the year before Shakespeare at Hartshill and was brought up as a page in the house of Sir Henry Goodere. Goodere's daughter, Anne, was the love of Drayton's life, inspiring much of his poetry. But she married Sir Henry Rainsford of Clifford Chambers and Drayton remained a bachelor until his death. He had an education similar to Shakespeare and both were drawn to London as young men. Once there they moved in the same circles as successful playwrights and poets. The managers, patrons, actors, and writers who created the London theatre were a tight though constantly shifting group in the early days, and the world of published poets was equally small. In the Theatre or the Rose or the Globe or the Fortune, with Philip Henslowe or Ben Jonson, Edward Alleyn or the Burbages, or at the bookstores and printers near St. Paul's, Shakespeare and Drayton would undoubtedly have crossed paths.

Drayton wrote for the theatre for about ten years, in particular collaborating with other writers on about twenty plays for producer

Philip Henslowe's Admiral's Men between 1597 and 1602. Francis Meres, in his 1598 *Palladis Tamia, Wit's Treasury*, listed "honey-tongued" Shakespeare of the Chamberlain's Men as the only play-wright excellent in both comedy and tragedy, but "golden-mouthed" Michael Drayton was one of Shakespeare's rivals for tragedy.[23] Though Meres lists more play titles for Shakespeare, he quotes Drayton more frequently. The competitive nature of these two men would have heightened their interest in one another.

In 1599 Drayton collaborated on the historical play *Sir John Old-castle*, countering Shakespeare's depiction of Oldcastle as Falstaff in *Henry IV*. After 1602 Drayton turned to the serious poetry on which his reputation is now based, and for this work he counted among his patrons the princely sons of James I, the Countess of Bedford, the Earl and Countess of Dorset, and the Rainsfords, with whom he often stayed in Clifford Chambers. Having started as a published poet in 1593 with *Idea: The Shepherd's Garland* (nine pastoral poems), in 1594 he added *Idea's Mirror*, sixty-four sonnets addressed to Idea, the symbolic name for his beloved Anne Goodere. An experimenter in form, he wrote *Poems Lyrical and Pastoral* (1605) (containing his dra-matic poem, the *Ballad of Agincourt*); *Heroical Epistles* (1597–1599) a series of love letters in verse between historical personages; and *Polyobion* (1612), which takes the geography of England as its subject and consists of thirty songs, each containing about four hundred lines of hexameter couplets about English history and myths.

Drayton wrote for the theatre the way most playwrights of the era did: as one of several collaborators churning out a play that would be sold outright to a company for a small amount. To get by, a writer had to write constantly and be prepared to take whatever collabora-tors or subjects came to hand, dependent on what a producer wanted for his company and felt he could sell to the public. It was even harder then than it is now to make a living as a writer. Michael Drayton attempted to found a production company with Martin Slater, who was an actor at one time with the Admiral's Men, a manager, and a self-described citizen and ironmonger. Together they established a boys' troupe called the Children of the King's Revels at the White-friar's. It was not a success. Slater returned as an actor to Queen Anne's Men and he struggled financially.

Even Shakespeare would have had a difficult time making a living had he remained just a writer. The difference in their fortunes was attributable, first, to the fact that Shakespeare, unlike Drayton, was a good actor, hired into an excellent company, which gave him a stable income and connections. Second, he had gained enough money, perhaps through Southampton's rewards for his epic poems, and was compatible enough with the other owners, to buy a place as a shareholder in the acting company (then the Chamberlain's Men). Following this, the popularity of the plays he wrote had a direct impact on the income of the shareholders. Finally, his canny business sense led him to good investments (particularly in Stratford real estate and tithes). None of these skills or opportunities had been available to his friend Michael Drayton.

Drayton the poet was prolific, well-connected, widely published, and admired, yet he ended his life an impoverished bachelor, his last five pounds lying beside him at his death.

The Davenant Family

John Davenant ?–1622
Jane Davenant ?–1622
William Davenant 1606–1668

> Go, sirrah, take them to the buttery,
> And give them friendly welcome every one—
> Let them want nothing that my house affords.
> *The Taming of the Shrew*, Induction, scene 1

Shakespeare's journeys from Stratford to London often took him through Oxford. This university town was on a main road that Shakespeare traveled dozens of times, whether on tour with his company or visiting his family. The ninety-mile trip would take at least two days each way, and regular stops in Oxford solidified Shakespeare's friendship with the Davenant family.

The Davenants owned the Crown Tavern, a wine house and inn in Oxford. John Davenant, who was to become mayor of Oxford, was a notably melancholy man never known to laugh. He was married to a very beautiful lady named Jane who was reputed to be witty and of sprightly conversation. Shakespeare was godfather to their son William and he visited often enough that another of the Davenants' seven children, Robert, later remembered being showered with a hundred kisses by the London playwright.

According to Aubrey in his *Brief Lives*, godson William Davenant wished to establish an even closer relationship with Shakespeare. William went on to become the most prominent theatre impresario in London at the end of the century, and in adulthood liked to claim that Shakespeare was his actual father. He cheerfully claimed this connection to the great man in spite of its obvious effect on the reputation of his mother, who, it should be said, was widely regarded as a virtuous wife. To substantiate the claimed connection, William noted a similarity in appearance between his famous godfather and himself. Nevertheless, anyone comparing their portraits today must credit William Davenant with a fine imagination indeed.

Friends at Work

❧ ❧

Where We Explore Shakespeare's Friendships in the Hectic
World of the Elizabethan/Jacobean Theatre

When Shakespeare arrived in London in the late 1580s, the theatre
scene was enlivened by three vibrant personalities: Philip Henslowe, a theatre manager; Edward Alleyn, the greatest rhetorical actor of
the time; and Christopher Marlowe who, though younger than Shakespeare, was revolutionizing the theatre experience with his plays. None of
these men was Shakespeare's close friend, and he left nothing to Henslowe or Alleyn in his will. Yet Shakespeare worked with them all; they
went beyond mere acquaintance. He knew them well, they influenced his
writing, and knowledge of them illuminates Shakespeare's life.

Philip Henslowe (?–1616)

What is the figure? What is the figure?
Love's Labours Lost, act 5, scene 1

I will draw up a list of properties such as our play wants.
A Midsummer Night's Dream, act 1, scene 2

Scholars owe a great debt to the meticulous bookkeeper Philip Henslowe. He kept what is called a diary, but is in reality a ledger, registering in detail the minute daily monetary transactions of his theatre company and other businesses. From his entry of October 16, 1599, we know about Michael Drayton's collaborative work and modest remuneration. It reads: "Received by me Thomas Downton of Philip Henslowe, to pay Mr. Munday, Mr. Drayton, Mr. Wilson, and Hathway, for The first part of the Lyfe of Sir John Ouldcastell, and in earnest of the Second Pte, for the use of the company, ten pound."[1] The precision of his accounting, contrasted to the casual spelling and punctuation (variable spellings were typical at the time), would be a distinguishing feature of Henslowe's records and of the nature of his personality.

From the diary we know that the property inventory of the Admiral's Men was augmented with the following purchase: "sewtes (suits?), ... Cupedes bowe and quiver, ... the clothe of the Sone and Mone, j rocke, j cage, j Hell-mought, j tome of Dido, j bedstead"[2]— tiny factual details that conjure up pictures of Elizabethan backstage life and onstage productions.

But theatre was not Henslowe's only business. A jack of all trades, he worked first for the bailiff of the Liberty of the Clink (1577) where he established the residence he kept for the rest of his life. As he married Agnes Woodward (his master's widow) about this time, he most probably was born no later than the mid-1550s, the son of Edmund Henslowe of Lindfield, Sussex, a master gamekeeper. But a country life was not for son Philip. The city drew him and he dove into many of the sleazy businesses thriving on Bankside: once claiming to be a dyer, he became a pawnbroker, owner of brothels and tenements, and active in the bearbaiting business. In this, his title (an ironic nod to his father) was Master of the Game of Paris Garden. He was careful to establish a veneer of respectability, becoming a Groom of the Chamber (1603, a recognition from the new King James I) and Sewer of the Chamber as well as a governor of the local grammar school and a church warden at St. Savior's, Southwark.

In 1587 he built the first theatre on Bankside, the Rose, and by 1594 owned the theatre at Newington Butts. Later he would help to build the Fortune and the Hope. The Hope housed both theatre productions and bearbaiting exhibitions, symbolic of the dichotomy in Henslowe's personality. The great actor Edward Alleyn married Henslowe's stepdaughter Joan in 1592, which solidified Henslowe's connection with the Admiral's Men, a distinguished and profitable theatre company second only to Shakespeare's Chamberlain's Men.

The first entry in Henslowe's diary is from February 1591 and in it he records productions and revenues of Lord Strange's Men. The fourth play mentioned in his first list is a performance of *Henry VI* on March 3, thus establishing the first known link between Shakespeare, Lord Strange's Men, and Philip Henslowe.

By 1595 Shakespeare had allied himself permanently with the Burbages and the Lord Chamberlain's Men. For a year or so the Rose theatre was just a few steps from the Globe and there must have been encounters, acknowledgements, and exchanges between the meticulous but raffish Philip Henslowe and the increasingly distinguished William Shakespeare. Shortly after the turn of the seventeenth century, Henslowe moved to his new theatre north of town and the easy encounters between theatre professionals on the same piece of land ended.

Philip Henslowe's tightfisted, hardheaded business practices brought retribution. In 1615 a group of actors from Lady Elizabeth's Company (combined with the Queen's Revels and Prince Charles's Company) drew up an accusation of oppression, accusing Mr. "Hinchlowe" (creative spelling again) of not paying ten pounds owed them and, "Also wee have paid him for plaie bookes 200 pounds or thereaboutes and yet hee denies to give us the Coppies of any one of them. Also within three yeares hee hadt broken and dismembered five Companies."[3]

No one would have wished for bearbaiting at the Globe, or desired a closer friendship between the crafty owner of stews and tenements and the gentlemanly owner of New Place, Stratford. But what wouldn't we give for a diarist like Henslowe from the Chamberlain's/King's Men, and Henslowe-like records from the Globe?

Edward Alleyn (1566–1626)

Not Rocius nor Aesope, those admired tragedians that have lived ever since before Christ was born, could ever performe more in action than famous Ned Alleyn.

Pierce Penilesse (1592), Thomas Nash

Edward Alleyn, the greatest rhetorical actor of the Elizabethan stage, rose to great wealth and distinction in life. Partnered with Philip Henslowe in a number of theatre managements, Edward Alleyn profited, like Shakespeare, more from investment in real estate and entertainment ventures than from his artistic genius.

A devoted husband, Alleyn had two famous fathers-in-law: Philip Henslowe, the stepfather of his first wife Joan, to whom he was married for most of his adult life, and the great poet John Donne, who was the father of his second wife.

To Joan, his twenty-two-year-old newlywed wife, the great actor (age twenty-seven) wrote on tour in 1593:

> My good sweet Mouse, I commend me heartily to you, and to my father, my mother, and my sister Bess, hoping in God, though the sickness be round about you, yet by his mercy it may escape your house.... Therefore use this course: keep your house fair and clean, which I know you will, and every evening throw water before your door and in your back side, and have in your windows good store of rue and herb of grace....
>
> Mouse, you send me no news of anything; you should send me of your domestical matters, such things as happen at home, as how your distilled water proves, or this, or that, or any thing what you will.
>
> And Jug, I pray you, let my orange tawny stockings of wool be dyed a very good black against I come home, to wear in the winter. You sent me not a word of my garden but next time you will. But remember this in any case, that all that bed which was parsley, in the month of September you sow with spinach, for then is the time. I would do it myself, but we shall not come home till All-Hallowstide. And so sweet Mouse, farewell—and brook our long journey with patience.[4]

Henslowe complained that Alleyn didn't write to his wife as often as other actors wrote to theirs, indicating how much most of the peripatetic Elizabethan actors treasured their wives and families. Alleyn did write, however. In addition to his own letters, he sent home to his wife a letter dictated to him by his apprentice who was traveling with the acting company. Training apprentices was an accepted job for successful actors, and these apprentices lived with and became part of the family. In the letter from Alleyn's apprentice, salutations were sent to everyone in the household, including servants Dolly (who woke him in the morning), Sara, in charge of cleaning his shoes, and an old man who contested him for the seat in the chimney corner. The apprentice's name was John Pyk, who signed himself, "your petty, pretty, prattling, parleying pig."[5]

Living alone in his rented London rooms, Shakespeare missed out on the busy domesticity, the house filled with wife, children, servants, and apprentices, that so enriched the home life of his London colleagues. Surely he wrote to his family, but all communication between Shakespeare's London and Stratford households has been lost.

Edward Alleyn was born right in London, the son of an innkeeper who was also porter to the queen. He started acting at a very young age. Before he had turned eighteen he was a member of Worcester's Men, and not long afterwards he joined the Admiral's Men, where his brother John was also an actor. There, he was soon playing the great roles written for the Admiral's company by Christopher Marlowe: Tamberlaine in *Tamberlaine the Great*, Faustus in *Dr. Faustus*, Barabas in *The Jew of Malta*. Tall, handsome, and with a remarkable voice, Edward Alleyn thrilled audiences with his interpretation of Marlowe's thundering language. Though some critics argue that Shakespeare was criticizing Alleyn's operatic acting style in Hamlet's advice to the players (warning them not to "out Herod Herod" or to "saw the air with their hands"), given Alleyn's reputation it is more likely the satire was directed at his less-gifted fellows. Or perhaps it was directed at Alleyn's replacement. At about the time that *Hamlet* was conceived, Alleyn had retired as an actor. Queen Elizabeth was so displeased at Alleyn's leaving the stage, however, that he was compelled to return. His career as an actor was therefore split into two parts: from the early 1580s until he retired in about 1597, and from 1600 to 1604.

The time Shakespeare and Alleyn most likely spent together was from 1590 to 1594. At this time Alleyn led a company that combined actors from the Admiral's Men and Lord Strange's Men. The company included actors William Kemp, Thomas Pope, John Heminges, Augustin Phillips, and George Bryan, all of whom were members of the Lord Chamberlain's company in future years. Although Shakespeare himself was not yet listed as a player, Alleyn's company's list of plays performed included a *Henry VI*, the one assumed to be Shakespeare's first work.

In 1594, the year Shakespeare became a shareholder in the Lord Chamberlain's Men, Edward Alleyn was both actor and partner in the Admiral's Men. The companies were highly competitive. The year after the newly built Globe set the standard for new theatres (1599) Edward Alleyn and Philip Henslowe built the Fortune, across the river in the northern suburbs. They hired Peter Street, the builder of the Globe, and asked him to build a theatre in the Globe style, but square instead of circular (Alleyn's request). This experiment was not successful and years later, after the Fortune had been damaged by a fire, their rebuilt theatre returned to the old, rounded form.

Even Alleyn's second departure from acting was at an early age. At forty-two his retirement left the title of "greatest actor of the day" to Richard Burbage. When his wife Joan died nineteen years later, in 1623, he wooed Constance Donne, daughter of the famous poet and dean of St. Paul's. John Donne was not eager for the marriage. However, while Constance came with a dowry of just 500 pounds, wealthy and successful Edward Alleyn was able to settle on her three times that amount, and she had a trust of 1,500 pounds when Alleyn died three years after their marriage.

In 1609, five years after retiring from the stage, Alleyn records in a diary that he spent sixpence to purchase the newly printed *Sonnets* of Shakespeare. No other document records the sale of this book, which received little notice and disappeared almost immediately. There was no subsequent printing for over a hundred years. As the sonnets were published seemingly without Shakespeare's knowledge or permission, and since they included hints and references possibly damaging to important people (such as the now highly respectable Earl of Southampton), and revelations of emotions and relationships embarrassing to Shakespeare himself, it is thought the book was suppressed. As a result, there are only thirteen copies still extant from this printing, making the quarto of the *Sonnets* infinitely more valuable than copies of the First Folio of Shakespeare's plays, of which there remain about two hundred (though only fourteen are in perfect condition). The degree to which the *Sonnets* are autobiographical, the mysterious Mr. W. H. to whom the printer, Thomas Thorpe, referred in his dedication page, the identities of the beautiful young man, the rival poet, and the Dark Lady are mysteries that attract scholars to this day. Alleyn might have had opinions on the mysterious identities of people in the sonnets as he most probably knew the individuals involved. Alas, he left no record of his reactions. Besides, the book was ancient history: the sonnet fad was over, and Shakespeare's poems published in 1609 probably dealt with events fifteen or more years in the past.

Alleyn was the wealthiest of the Elizabethan actors. While many of them—most in Shakespeare's company—became well-off, respected property owners and model citizens, Alleyn amassed a huge fortune and received a coat of arms connecting him with the Townley family of Lancashsire. Childless, yet eager that his name be remembered, he established a number of almshouses and then founded and endowed a college. To do this he bought the manor of Dulwich after he retired from acting in 1604. He then spent 10,000 pounds to buy the rest of the estate and moved there in 1613 to build the College of God's Gift, now Dulwich College, which opened in 1619. Furthermore, he decreed that the master and warden of the College should always bear his own name. Though this was not always possible, graduates of Dulwich College to this day call themselves "Old Alleynians." Edward Alleyn never lost the urge to invest in property and died of a chill caught while he was visiting some land in Yorkshire that he had recently acquired.

When people visit the remarkable art collection at Dulwich College they'll find more portraits of Elizabethan actors than in any other locale. They will also find within the library walls the papers of Edward Alleyn and Christopher Marlowe, friends of Shakespeare's youth, and two of England's greatest theatre artists.

Christopher Marlowe (1564–1593)

Marlowe, bathed in the Thespian springs,
Had in him those brave translunary things
That our first poets had: his raptures were
All air and fire, which made his verses clear:
For that fine madness still he did retain
Which rightly should possess a poet's brain.

Elegies Upon Sundry Occasions, Michael Drayton

When Shakespeare arrived in London, young Christopher Marlowe was the city's leading playwright, the most thrilling of the university wits who dazzled London audiences with verbal fireworks, inventing an entirely new theatrical language. So powerful was his personality and influence that, in *Shakespeare: The Invention of the Human*, Harold Bloom suggests the ghost of Christopher Marlowe haunted all of Shakespeare's early writing life. Marlowe was born in Canterbury two months before Shakespeare. Those thinking Shakespeare, whose father was a glover, had a parentage too lowly to account for his genius must confront the fact that the other two great Elizabethan playwrights, Christopher Marlowe and Ben Jonson, were the sons, respectively, of a shoemaker and a bricklayer.

Intellectually precocious, Marlowe graduated from Cambridge with a B.A. in 1584 and an M.A. in 1587. While still in school he had written *Tamburlaine the Great*, produced that same year (1587) with young Edward Alleyn stirring audiences as the great conqueror. Algernon Charles Swinburne, in his article for the *Encyclopedia Britannica* of 1911 observed of Marlowe:

> He is the greatest discoverer, the most daring and inspired pioneer, in all our poetic literature. Before him there was neither genuine blank verse nor a genuine tragedy in our language. After his arrival the way was prepared, the paths were made straight, for Shakespeare.[6]

The paths may have been straight, but no two personalities could have been more divergent.

Marlowe, the rebellious, atheistic intellectual, took up with Walter Raleigh, who had gathered around him a group of liberal, vociferous freethinkers. Among these was Thomas Kyd, another playwright, known for his atheism. In 1593 Marlowe was arrested and accused of having papers containing "vile heretical conceits denying the divinity of Jesus Christ."[7] Marlowe said the papers were Kyd's, but Kyd claimed they were Marlowe's. Kyd was imprisoned, but Marlowe died before he could be incarcerated.

In his brief life Marlowe wrote reams of poetry. One of his light verses leaps over the centuries:

The Passionate Shepherd to His Love

Come live with me and be my Love,
And we will all the pleasures prove
That hills and valleys, dales and fields,
Or woods or steepy mountain yields.

And we will sit upon the rocks,
And see the shepherds feed their flocks
By shallow rivers, to whose falls
Melodious birds sing madrigals.

And I will make thee beds of roses
And a thousand fragrant posies;
A cap of flowers, and a kirtle
Emboider'd all with leaves of myrtle.

A gown maide of the finest wool
Which from our pretty lambs we pull;
Fair-lined slippers for the cold,
With buckles of the purest gold.

A belt of straw and ivey-buds
With coral clasps and amber studs.
And if these pleasures may thee move
Come live with me and be my love.

The shepherd swains shall dance and sing
For thy delight each May morning:
If these delights thy mind may move,
Then live with me and be my Love.[8]

Though he wrote and published an astonishing amount of poetry, he remains best known for his plays, *Tamburlaine the Great* (two parts), *Dr. Faustus*, *The Jew of Malta*, *Edward II*, *The Massacre at Paris*, and *Dido, Queen of Carthage*, core works of the Admiral's Men's repertory (Edward Alleyn's reputation was based on his portrayal of Marlowe's lead characters in these plays).

Marlowe's language is glorious. In *Dr. Faustus* he says of Helen of Troy:

Was this the face that launched a thousand ships
And burnt the topless towers of Ilium?
Sweet Helen, make me immortal with a kiss.
    (Kisses her)
Her lips suck forth my soul; see where it flies!—
Come, Helen, come, give me my soul again.
Here will I dwell, for Heaven is in these lips,
And all is dross that is not Helena...
Oh, thou art fairer than the evening air
Clad in the beauty of a thousand stars.[9]

His portrait of Faustus as he faces death uses language to reveal psychological torment:

Ah, Faustus,
Now hast thou but one bare hour to live,
And then thou must be damned perpetually!

> Stand still, you ever-moving spheres of Heaven,
> That time may cease, and midnight never come.
> Fair Nature's eye, rise, rise again and make
> Perpetual day; or let this hour be but
> A year, a month, a week, a natural day,
> That Faustus may repent and save his soul!
> O lente, lente, currite noctis equi!
> The stars move still, time runs, the clock will strike
> The Devil will come, and Faustus must be damned.[10]

Marlowe's own death was the result of his volatile, risk-taking behavior. At age twenty-nine he was stabbed to death in a Deptford inn, ostensibly because of a quarrel over the bill. As evidence exists connecting Marlowe to espionage for the crown, there has been speculation that his death was politically arranged. Ingram Frizer, the man accused of the murder, was judged to have acted in self-defense and was pardoned, but those who favor the espionage scenario feel his acquittal was a cover-up.

Bloom finds Marlowe echoed everywhere in Shakespeare's early plays, *Titus Andronicus* being Shakespeare's effort to out-do Marlowe (and Kyd, for that matter) in writing over-the-top revenge drama. Bloom further considers Marlowe to be the inspiration for Edmund in as late a play as *King Lear*.

In *The Merry Wives of Windsor*, Shakespeare has his pedantic Sir Hugh Evans singing a song with the refrain "melodious birds sing madrigals," quoted directly from Marlowe's poem about the passionate shepherd. In *As You Like It*, Shakespeare alludes to Marlowe's death twice, and has Phoebe quote from Marlowe:

> Now dead poet I know thy saw of might
> "Whoever loved that loved not at first sight."[11]

Yet it was on stentorian, oratorical outbursts that Marlowe's fame rested.

> Tamburlaine
> The host of Xerxes, which by fame is said
> To have drank the mighty Parthian Araris,
> Was but a handful to that we will have.
> Our quivering lances, shaking in the air,
> And bullets, like Jove's dreadful thunderbolts,
> Inrolled in flames and fiery smouldering mists,

Shall threat the gods more than Cyclopian wars:
And with our sun-bright armour as we march,
We'll chase the stars from Heaven and dim their eyes
That stand and muse at our admired arms.[12]

Scholars who identify Marlowe as the rival poet of Shakespeare in his *Sonnets* recognize he was the only poet of his day Shakespeare could have held in awe. Yet Shakespeare did not need to feel intimidated by Marlowe's genius, as Bloom suggests. Where Marlowe wrote his title roles for the oratorical abilities of Edward Alleyn, Shakespeare wrote for the humanity revealed in the acting of Richard Burbage, and included in his plays vivid portraits of the common man. Where Marlowe blazed new light on the stage, Shakespeare cast more varied and interesting shadows. And where Marlowe thundered out reams of sublime tragic pentameters, Shakespeare proved in his history plays that he could write such drama just as well. What's more, Shakespeare could make his audiences laugh. Most innovative of all, Shakespeare created out of language what Marlowe could not: characters who seem like living, breathing human beings.

Ben Jonson (1572–1637)

O rare Ben Jonson
                    Ben Jonson's monument, Westminster Abbey

Drink to me only with thine eyes
And I will pledge with mine.
Or leave a kiss within the cup
And I'll not ask for wine
The thirst that from the soul doth rise
Doth ask a drink divine.
But might I of Jove's nectar sup
I would not change for thine.

I sent thee late a rosy wreath
Not so much honoring thee
As giving it a hope that there

It could not withered be.
But thou thereon did'st only breathe
And send'st it back to me
Since when it grows and smells, I swear
Not of itself, but thee.[13]

Ben Jonson's most famous lyric (like Christopher Marlowe's) gives little hint of his bellicose nature. The poem by George Chapman that Marchette Chute uses to introduce her biography *Ben Jonson of Westminster* comes closer to suggesting Jonson's robust character:

Give me a spirit that on this life's rough sea
Loves t'have his sails filled with a lusty wind
Even till his sail-yards tremble, his masts crack,
And his rapt ship runs on her side so low
That she drinks water and her keel plows air.[14]

Jonson was born in 1572 in Westminster, which was not at that time a part of London. His father died before he was born, and soon after his mother married a master bricklayer. Jonson was brilliant from the time of his youth, and his mother was able to enter him at Westminster School where he studied with William Camden, a man to whom Jonson expressed gratitude for his education all his life. After leaving Westminster School, however, Jonson's erudition was achieved on his own. Lacking a scholarship to Cambridge—a bitter and hard-to-understand failure—Jonson was apprenticed to his stepfather and applied himself for the entire seven years, working as a bricklayer. Jonson despised the trade, however, and left to join the army where he served in England's war in the Netherlands.

By then he had married a young London woman named Anne Lewis. The marriage must have been difficult, as Jonson described her as "a shrew, but honest,"[15] while he announced himself "given to venery"[16] and seemed proud both of his female conquests and his frequent duels. Perhaps this is why Jonson and his wife separated for five years.

The couple reconciled, however, and had several children of whom at least three died. One was baby Mary, whom Jonson and his wife grieved over as "the daughter of their youth."[17] Their seven-year-old son Ben died of the plague, and Jonson wrote movingly:

Farewell, thou child of my right hand, and joy;
My sin was too much hope of thee, loved boy . . .

Rest in soft peace, and asked, say, "Here doth lie
Ben Jonson his best piece of poetry."[18]

A second son (also named Ben) died when he was three. Ben Jonson was able to channel his grief into lovely, heartfelt poems, revealing the depth of his loss. Shakespeare, on the death of his son, found relief only in the deepening treatment of themes of time, loss, and mortality in his plays. Jonson's love of children also found expression in the plays he wrote for the boys' acting companies, where two young actors were especially close to him: Nathan Field, who became his pupil and acted in many of his plays, and Solomon Pavy who, like Jonson's own sons, died at a young age (thirteen). For Pavy, Jonson wrote:

Weep with me, all you that read
This little story,
And know, for whom a tear you shed,
Death's self is sorry.[19]

Jonson's war service in the Netherlands proved that he was no more cut out to be a soldier than a bricklayer. It was when he came home to London from the war in 1597 that he changed the spelling of his name from the more typical "Johnson" and began to work as an actor and playwright. He immediately landed in trouble. Having helped Thomas Nashe write a seditious play, *The Isle of Dogs*, he and two other actors from Pembroke's Men (Robert Shaw and Gabriel Spencer) were clapped into Marshalsea prison while all the theatres were closed for a day. The meticulous Philip Henslowe noted in his diary of July 28, 1597, a loan of four pounds to the imprisoned Ben Jonson. Perhaps Henslowe's loan kept Jonson occupied with pens, ink, and paper, writing plays in jail until his release the following October.

The next year Jonson killed in a duel the same Gabriel Spencer who had been his fellow in prison. Incarcerated in Newgate Prison, this time for murder, he escaped execution only by pleading benefit of clergy. He converted to Catholicism (another choice likely to get him into trouble in Protestant England), and kept to that faith for twelve years.

At first Jonson wrote plays for Henslowe and the Admiral's Company, for the Children of the Chapel, and later for the Chamberlain's/King's Men. Jonson kept records, as Shakespeare did not, of who acted in his plays, and these lists have helped our understanding of what kind of parts Shakespeare and the other members of the company played. Nicholas Rowe, the early-eighteenth-century Shakespearean enthusiast and scholar, claims that the Shakespeare-Jonson friendship began when Shakespeare persuaded the King's Men to accept Jonson's comedy *Every Man in His Humour* for production in 1598 (shortly after Jonson's imprisonment). Shakespeare is listed as a prominent member of the cast and another early biographer, Thomas Fuller (1643–1681), claims that there were many "wit-combates betwixt him and Ben Jonson."[20]

As his infidelities undoubtedly tried his marriage, Jonson's arrogance, conceit, and lack of tact irritated his professional colleagues. From 1600 to 1602 he disputed publicly with Thomas Dekker and John Marston in the "War of the Theatres" (the quarrel Dekker called "Poetomachia"). During this time, Jonson, in his play *Poetaster*, had the boy actors satirize adult writers and actors, criticizing Dekker and Marston in particular. Dekker riposted with his *Satiromastix*, in which he gives us a portrait of the Ben Jonson of 1601: he reminds the audience of Jonson's plebeian background as a bricklayer and touring actor, as a seditious playwright and a murderer. He tells us that Jonson was short and pockmarked. He derides Jonson's slowness in writing and makes fun of the faces Jonson made when reading his poetry aloud. Most of all, Dekker satirizes Jonson's ambition and conceit. Despite this critical portrait, Dekker was more amiable than cruel and the "war" burnt itself out. Jonson, however, was later called before the royal council, accused of treason and popery in his tragedy *Sejanus*, and in 1609 was imprisoned once again—this time for ridiculing the Scots (a sensitive topic with a Scottish-born king on the throne) in *Eastward, Ho!* Jonson's contentious public life was a complete contrast to Shakespeare's. No wonder in *3 Parnassus* (1605) an anonymous Cambridge playwright wrote, "O that Ben Jonson is a pestilent fellow."[21]

Jonson and Shakespeare approached playwriting from opposite ends of the spectrum. While Shakespeare poured out instinctive works filled with characters expressing individual and often contradictory points of view, Jonson was a polemicist. He (like George Bernard Shaw three hundred years later) saw the theatre as a platform to express ideas. Jonson applied the popular Renaissance philosophy of "humours" to the creation of his characters. Characters were developed as exemplars of the effect on human personality of phlegmatic, melancholic, choleric, or sanguine bodily fluids, which the scientists of the age claimed determined human character. Furthermore, following the *Poetics* of Renaissance scholar Julius Caesar Scaliger and the writings of Sir Philip Sidney, Jonson, the theorist, insisted that comedy had to be based in realism, not fantasy, and should have a didactic purpose. Comedy was supposed to criticize and improve human behavior. Shakespeare's *As You Like It* and *Twelfth Night, or What You Will* by their very titles must have seemed an affront to Jonson's need for moral purpose. *The Tempest*'s Ariel and *A Midsummer Night's Dream*'s fairies existed in a different universe from Jonson's *Volpone, The Alchemist,* and *Bartholomew Fair*. Fortunately, in plays like these, Jonson's genius coincided with his theory, and, though very different from Shakespeare, these great works, given great productions, can be as satisfying today as when first performed. Jonson's Senecan-based tragedies, however—*Cataline* and *Sejanus* (in which Shakespeare acted)—have not withstood the test of time and were found tedious even in his own era.

Ben Jonson was not gifted enough (or perhaps not interested enough) as an actor to become, like Shakespeare, a shareholding member of a stable company. He was, however, able to create and sustain relationships with members of the aristocracy. Ironically, despite his bellicose, opinionated, didactic temperament, much of his living was made writing and producing masques for the court. He must not have considered masques proper, serious drama as the fanciful, spectacular music and dance entertainment freely dealt with unrealistic gods, goddesses, and mythological subjects. They featured stunning scenery and costumes often designed by Jonson's friend Inigo Jones, and they were written to be performed by enthusiastic, aristocratic amateurs, even including the queen. Intellectual in content but superficial in nature, focusing on the externals of set design and costume, these masques lacked the profundity, the subtlety, the heart, that Shakespeare revealed in the plays he wrote for professional actors on the popular stage.

In addition to his seventeen plays and twenty-two masques, Jonson wrote poems, epigrams, scripts for public entertainment, and two prose books: *English Grammar* and *Timber, or Discoveries*. Many of his poems were addressed to his aristocratic patrons who gave Jonson continued support.

Jonson did the world an unwitting favor when he published a folio version of his plays in 1616. No writer had ever done such a thing before, and he was mocked for his pride. Plays that had a certain popularity and might generate sales were often issued in official or pirated versions as cheap paperback quartos. No one, however, considered a play script to be the kind of literature worthy of fine, expensive printing. By valuing his own work at this level, Jonson may have inspired Heminges and Condell to collect and print Shakespeare's plays in the First Folio, a treasure perhaps not imaginable without Jonson's example.

At the end of his life, Jonson was given a royal pension of 100 marks a year, becoming the first (though unofficial) British poet laureate. When he died in 1637 he was regarded as the leading figure of British literature. He remained a contentious personality, however: six years before his death, Jonson quarreled with the designer Inigo Jones, losing a friend and the partner with whom he created most of his royal masques.

Despite their wildly different personalities, Ben Jonson and William Shakespeare were and remained good friends. In fact, no one in this combative age ever seemed to have sustained a quarrel with William Shakespeare. Jonson was the only one we know who teased his friend Shakespeare publicly. When Shakespeare at last received the coat of arms he had requested for his father and thereby established himself as a gentleman, the family motto he chose was "Not without right." In *Everyman Out of His Humour*, performed the same year (1599), the iconoclastic Jonson (undoubtedly with a thrill of mischief) gave one of his characters the motto "Not without mustard."

While Shakespeare lived in London apart from his family, Jonson was married to (though he sometimes lived away from) the wife of his youth. But Jonson's loss of his children was one his friend Shakespeare could well understand as Shakespeare had suffered such loss when his eleven-year-old Hamnet died. And it was Jonson who, by report, traveled with Michael Drayton to Stratford to see Shakespeare, thereby hastening Shakespeare's death by allowing him to drink too much at this "merry meeting."

In Jonson we have at last a close friend of Shakespeare's who repeatedly expressed opinions about him in writing. Jonson reminisces in *Timber, or Discoveries*:

> I remember, the Players have often mentioned it as an honour to Shakespeare, that in his writing (whatsoever he penn'd) he never blotted out a line. My answer hath been, would he had blotted a thousand. Which they thought a malevolent speech. I had not told posterity this, but for their ignorance, who choose that circumstance to commend their friend by, wherein he most faulted. And to justify my own candour (for I lov'd the man, and do honour his memory (on this side idolatry) as much as any.) He was (indeed) honest, and of an open, and free nature: he had an excellent Phantsie; brave notions, and gentle expressions: wherein he flow'd with that facility, that sometime it was necessary he should be stopp'd: *Sufflaminandus erat*; as Augustus said of Haterius. His wit was in his own power; would the rule of it had been so too. Many

times he fell into those things, could not escape laughter: As when he said in the person of Caesar, one speaking to him: "Caesar thou dost me wrong." He replied: "Caesar did never wrong, but with just cause." and such like: which were ridiculous. But he redeemed his vices, with his virtues. There was ever more in him to be praised, than to be pardoned.[22]

When asked to write an introductory poem for the First Folio of Shakespeare's plays, where the purpose was to praise, Jonson revealed his powers of appreciation and his own generous heart in verses to his friend:

> Soul of the age!
> The applause! delight! the wonder of our stage!
> My Shakespeare, rise. I will not lodge thee by
> Chaucer or Spenser or bid Beaumont lie
> A little further, to make thee a room;
> Thou are a monument without a tomb,
> And art alive still, while thy book doth live,
> And we have wits to read, and praise to give. . . .
> Triumph, my Britain, thou hast one to show
> To whom all scenes of Europe homage owe.
> He was not of an age, but for all time.[23]

Each of these friends, so different yet so able to appreciate each other's work, found rest where he wanted to be: "gentle" Shakespeare in Trinity Church, near his family, in the small town he loved; "rare" Ben Jonson in Westminster Abbey with the great poets of England in the middle of its greatest city.

THE COLLABORATORS

Thomas Dekker
Francis Beaumont
John Fletcher

In the English renaissance theatre the play script authored by a single individual was rare compared to those turned out by committee. Like the early studio-controlled days of Hollywood filmmaking, writers were hired to get a script ready in a hurry. An author (like modern "play doctors") could be hired for very little money to improve an existing work; he could be hired with one other writer in a collaborative partnership, or he might be signed on as part of a team where each writer was responsible for a small part of the finished work. Some writers excelled in setting out the plot, some in writing dialogue, some in writing songs. If the producer were in real haste he could hire a different writer for each act.

Except for his very earliest and very latest plays (whose proportion of Shakespearean authorship scholars love to dispute), Shakespeare worked alone. He was able to do this because he was a shareholder in the company and therefore in a position to hire himself. Because he wrote quickly and efficiently, and because he was supremely gifted, he needed no help turning out superb and timely play scripts on his own.

On the rare occasions when he offered plays that seem to show more than one hand (*Pericles, Henry VIII*), the probability that Shakespeare worked with others must be acknowledged, for most Elizabethan/ Jacobean playwriting was done this way. Three of his contemporaries, all collaborators themselves, worked closely with the King's Men and therefore might be thought of as among Shakespeare's most likely writing partners and close writer-friends. These are Thomas Dekker, Francis Beaumont, and John Fletcher.

Thomas Dekker (c. 1572–c. 1632)

> Kind gentlemen and honest boon companions, I present you here
> with a merry-conceited Comedy. . . . Take all in good worth that is
> well intended, for nothing is purposed but mirth; mirth length-
> eneth long life, which, with all other blessings, I heartily wish you.
>
> Dedication to *The Shoemaker's Holiday*, Thomas Dekker

Thomas Dekker had need of his mirthful philosophy. He spent most of his life in poverty and six years or more in prison for debt. His dire straights never embittered him, however. His work is noted for its artlessness, simplicity, and endless, good-humored joy.

Little is known of Dekker's early life. Conjecture has it that he was born in London of a Dutch immigrant tailor, perhaps attended Merchant Tailor's School, and possibly served an apprenticeship as a cobbler or a tailor. In his early twenties he married, and by twenty-five was working on a play called *Fayeton* (Phaeton) for Philip Henslowe (who lists him as Mr. Dickers in his diary). The following year Henslowe was advancing forty shillings to get Dekker out of prison for debt. It was a good investment for Henslowe as Dekker wrote or collaborated on forty-four plays, primarily for Henslowe's company. The works include:

1599	*Troilus and Cressida*, with Henry Chettle
1599	*Robert the Second, King of Scots*, with Ben Jonson and Henry Chettle
1599	*The Shoemaker's Holiday*, sole author
1600	*Old Fortunatus*, sole author
1601	*Satiromastrix*, sole author
1604	*The Honest Whore* (first part), with Thomas Middleton
	Northward Ho, Westward Ho, with John Webster
	Sir Thomas Wyatt, with John Webster
1611	*The Roaring Girl*, with Thomas Middleton
1622	*The Virgin Martyr*, with Philip Massinger
	The Witch of Edmonton, with John Ford
1630	*The Honest Whore* (second part), with Thomas Middleton
1631	*Match Me in London*, sole author

Dekker's most lasting work is *The Shoemaker's Holiday*. A rollicking comedy, it lets one enter the lively, daily working life of Elizabethan London in the same way Shakespeare's *The Merry Wives of Windsor* lets us experience late-sixteenth-century country life.

From 1613 to 1616 Shakespeare was living the life of a country gentleman in a large house in Stratford. From 1613 to 1618 Dekker was in debtors' prison. There he turned from writing plays to writing devotions and prayers, a semi-autobiographical piece called *Dekker His Dream*, and a series of pamphlets that describe aspects of life in London at the time: "The Wonderful Year 1603" (describing the plague), "The Seven Deadly Sins of London," "News from Hell," and especially "The Gull's Hornbook," which satirically instructs a gauche young man on how to behave in the theatre, basing the advice on rude, thoughtless behaviors Dekker himself had observed in audiences. Dekker instructs the Gallant:

> Present not yourself on the Stage (especially at a new play) until the quaking prologue hath (by rubbing) got colour into his cheeks, and is ready to give the trumpets their Cue that he's upon point to enter; for then it is the time, as though you were one of the Properties, or that you dropt out of the Hangings, to creep from behind the Arras, with your Tripos or three-footed stool in one hand, and a teston mounted between a fore-finger and a thumb in the other. . . . It shall crown you with rich commendation to laugh aloud in the midst of the most serious and saddest scene of the terriblest Tragedy. . . . Before the Play begins, fall to cards . . . throw the cards (having first torn four or five of them) round about the Stage, just upon the third sound, as though you had lost. . . . Now, sir, if the writer be a fellow that hath . . . epigramd you . . . you shall disgrace him . . . if, in the middle of his play . . . you rise with a screud and discontented face from your stool and be gone: no matter whether the Scenes be good or no, the better they are the worse do you distaste them: and being on your feet, sneak not away like a coward, but salute all your gentle acquaintances, that are spread either on the rushes or on the stools about you, and draw what troop you can from the stage after you.[24]

Shakespeare and Dekker were two peaceable men of the theatre amidst a volatile and rowdy horde. Shakespeare avoided quarrels, but Dekker (partly because of his constant collaborations) became involved in the "war of the theatres" between John Marston and Ben Jonson, an exciting theatrical polemic which Dekker called the "Poetomachia."

The basis of this "war" was the umbrage each man took at what he believed (most often rightly) to be villainous representations of himself in plays of the other. Jonson bragged of quarrelling with Marston, of beating him, and of taking his pistol from him because of the way he believed Marston had represented him on stage as Christoganus in *Histriomastix*. Jonson got revenge by satirizing Marston's turgid writing style in *Everyman Out of His Humour*, after which Marston made Jonson a cuckold in his play *Jack Drum's Entertainment*.

In *The Poetaster* Jonson took on Dekker by making him Demetrius and ridiculing him as "a dresser of plays about town." Dekker replied with *Satiromastix*, which he wrote for the Chamberlain's Men (Shakespeare's company) and St. Paul's Children's company. After a couple of years, however, the conflict diffused and in 1604 Marston even dedicated his play *The Malcontent* to his old enemy Jonson.

Shakespeare refers to the "war of the theatres" in *Hamlet*, act 2, scene 2. Most of the Marston/Jonson/Dekker feuding plays were performed by boys' companies which were so popular that adult companies could not compete in London and were forced to take to the road. Shakespeare never wrote for the boy actors. His attitude toward them is clear in Rosencrantz's explanation to Hamlet of why the players who recently came to Elsinore are on tour:

> *Rosencrantz:* . . . there is, sir, an aery of children, little eyases, that cry out on the top of question, and are most tyrannically clapp'd for't. These are now the fashion and so berattle the common stages. . .that many wearing rapiers are afraid of goose-quills, and dare scarce come thither . . . .
> *Hamlet:* Do the boys carry it away?
> *Rosencrantz:* Ay, that they do my lord. . . .[25]

With these specific and acknowledged examples of playwrights using the stage—even the boys' stage—as a platform on which to pillory each other, it is no wonder Harold Bloom, in *Shakespeare: The Invention of the Human*, searches out portraits of Christopher Marlowe and Ben Jonson in Shakespeare's work. What is most curious is that Shakespeare is rarely, if ever, thought to have been the source for any part written by his numerous eager and contentious fellow writers. Though Shakespeare created unforgettably vivid personalities out of his prodigious imagination, no aspect of his own character or his life was so dominating, strong, identifiable, interesting, or pleading for satire that his colleagues longed to portray him. Parodying him did not interest them, and he eludes us, because he was just "gentle" Shakespeare.

The evidence of Dekker collaborations with Shakespeare is admittedly slight. A few critics find Dekker's hand as a "dresser" of plays in *Henry V* and *Julius Caesar*, both written during the late 1590s at the height of Dekker's activity in the theatre, but their evidence is internal and subjective. So it is possible that Dekker never dressed or doctored a Shakespeare play. But it is known that the two men were colleagues, and, given Dekker's sunny personality, we might hope they were friends.

Beaumont and Fletcher (1608–1613)

> An apple cleft in two is not more twin
> Than these two creatures.
>
> *Twelfth Night*, act 5, scene 1

In about 1608 a playwriting collaboration began between Francis Beaumont and John Fletcher, writing for the King's Men. It lasted five years and resulted in fifteen plays (tragi-comedies, tragedies, and romantic comedies) that were highly successful at the time of their writing. In the 1630s and again in the 1660s, the plays of Beaumont and Fletcher were far more popular than Shakespeare's work.

The two men might have been brought together by Beaumont's friend Ben Jonson, for whose *Volpone* both Beaumont and Fletcher wrote commendatory verses in 1607. They wrote seven plays for Queen Elizabeth's Company and for the court Revels, but most of their plays were written for the King's Men. Their engagement was undoubtedly tied to the King's Men's use of the Blackfriars Theatre, adapted to present professional adult plays in about 1608. The change in theatre space, from the outdoor, populist Globe to the indoor, private Blackfriars, heralded a change in playwriting subject and style, and marked a generational shift in the kind of plays produced from the time of early Shakespeare to the time of Beaumont and Fletcher. In addition to the style of their work, the upper-class origins of Beaumont and Fletcher made them desirable connections for the King's Men, who needed to attract a high-paying, aristocratic audience to the Blackfriars.

Until their collaboration, each writer had been only marginally successful, but once they started working together, their success skyrocketed. In the process they became extremely good friends. According to the gossipy John Aubrey, they "lived together on the Banke Side, not far from the Playhouse, both batchelors . . . had one wench in the house between them, which they did so admire" and had "the same cloathes and cloake . . . between them."[26] After their initial efforts, their most influential early work was *Philaster*, written for the King's Men in 1610, a tragi-comedy some liken to Shakespeare's *Cymbeline*.

Beaumont and Fletcher were the most important playwrights of the generation following Shakespeare, and their works include *Cupid's Revenge* (1608); *The Maid's Tragedy* and *Philaster* (1610); *Four Plays in One*, *The Coxcomb*, and *A King and No King* (1611); and *The Scornful Lady* (1613). The collaboration ended when Beaumont retired in 1613. Two folios of their work were published, illustrating just how prolific they were; the first in 1647 contained thirty-four plays and the second in 1679 contained fifty-two. Beaumont and Fletcher together were listed as the authors of all.

Francis Beaumont (1584–1616)

> Hold back thy hours, dark Night, till we have done;
> The Day will come too soon.
>
> *The Maid's Tragedy*, act 1, scene 2,
> Francis Beaumont and John Fletcher

Francis Beaumont was born in Grace Dieu Priory, Leicestershire, in 1584, twenty years after the birth of Shakespeare. He was the third and youngest son of a Sir Francis Beaumont, Justice of the Common Pleas. He seemed destined for a legal career like his father as he attended Pembroke College, Oxford (at that time Broadgates Hall) at thirteen; without taking a degree there, at the age of just sixteen, he was admitted to the Inner Temple. There he began writing poems, possibly encouraged by Michael Drayton, who was a friend of the family.

In his beginnings as a playwright, Beaumont established another valuable literary friendship with Ben Jonson, who took him on as a protege. In 1606 he wrote a comedy of humors (a Jonson specialty) called *The Woman Hater* for the Children of St. Paul's to perform, and in 1607 wrote the play for which he is best known: *The Knight of the Burning Pestle*. Though well remembered, this satire on the conventions of drama failed to please its first audiences. Beaumont's greatest successes would come after the next year when he began his collaboration with John Fletcher.

In 1615 a poem appeared addressed to Ben Jonson, written by FB, which we take to be Francis Beaumont:

> heere would I let slippe
> (If I had in mee) scholershippe
> And from all Learninge keepe these lines as clere
> As Shakespeare's best are, which our heires shall hear
> Preachers apte to their auditors to showe
> How farr sometimes a mortall man may goe
> By the dim light of nature.[27]

This educated man displays a very different attitude toward Shakespeare's work than the vicious Robert Greene, thirteen years before, who condemned Shakespeare's lack of university education. Greene claimed that it was only through university training and not by "the dim light of nature" that one could presume to write great works for the theatre.

In 1613, at twenty-nine, Francis Beaumont married an heiress, Ursula Isley. This same year he wrote his last work: a masque to be presented by the Inner Temple and Gray's Inn for Princess Elizabeth's wedding. Perhaps as a tribute to his great friend, John Fletcher took a scene from this masque and restaged it in his collaboration with Shakespeare, *The Two Noble Kinsmen*. Francis Beaumont died in March three years later, a month before Shakespeare died. At his death Francis Beaumont was only thirty-two years old. He is buried in Westminster Abbey near his mentor, Ben Jonson.

John Fletcher (1579–1625)

> Poets, when they rage,
> Turn gods to men, and make an hour an age.
>
> *The Maid's Tragedy*, act 1, scene 2,
> Francis Beaumont and John Fletcher

John Fletcher came from a distinguished family. His father was the vicar of Rye and later became bishop of Bristol, Worcester, and London. His Uncle Giles was a poet, a scholar, and a diplomat who was educated at Eton and King's College, Cambridge, where he was a fellow from 1568 to 1581 as a lecturer in Greek. A doctor in civil law, he became a member of Parliament in 1584. Giles was sent on a mission to Tsar Feodor Ivanovich in Russia, and when he returned he wrote an account, *Of the Russian Commonwealth*. He published a collection of sonnets in 1593, about the time Shakespeare was writing *Venus and Adonis* and perhaps some of his own sonnets. Two of Giles's sons, Phineas and Giles (John's cousins), were highly educated Anglican clergymen and well-known classical poets.

Though John Fletcher may have attended Corpus Christi College, Cambridge, in 1591, not much is known of his life before he began writing plays for the King's Men with Francis Beaumont in London in 1608. This collaboration was wildly successful and the two became the major English dramatists following Shakespeare's generation.

After Francis Beaumont married in 1613, the partnership broke up and the convivial Fletcher turned to other collaborators: Philip Massinger, William Rowley, George Chapman, Thomas Middleton, Ben Jonson, and most significantly, William Shakespeare. In addition, this prolific young man wrote about sixteen plays on his own. These included *Valentinian*, *Bonduck*, *Wit Without Money*, *The Island Princess* (a tragi-comedy following the pattern of *Philaster*, his great success with Beaumont in 1610), and *The Wild Goose Chase*, a comedy of manners that would influence the Restoration comedies at the end of the century.

Like Beaumont, Fletcher was influenced early in his career by Ben Jonson's comedies of humors, writing a number of fairly unsuccessful ones for the children's companies. His collaboration with Beaumont, and their friendship, led to a period of great productivity, however: fifteen popular plays in little more than five years (1608–1613).

With Shakespeare he is known to have written *The Two Noble Kinsmen* (in which he included the scene mentioned earlier, from Beaumont's masque for the wedding of Princess Elizabeth) and *Cardenio*. He also contributed a significant amount to Shakespeare's last play, *Henry VIII*, and succeeded him as the King's Men's leading dramatist. Shakespeare is not known to have worked so closely with any other dramatist. While collaboration was natural and stimulating for Fletcher, it seems Shakespeare collaborated only at the beginning and end of his career. In all likelihood, after Shakespeare announced his plan to leave the theatre and retire to Stratford, the King's Men pleaded with him for more plays. Perhaps he suggested a willingness only if someone helped with the work, and Fletcher, now the company's major playwright, was eager. But collaborating, it seems, did not rekindle Shakespeare's inspiration, and after *Henry VIII* he stopped writing altogether.

By the end of Fletcher's career, English Renaissance theatre had passed its zenith. William Shakespeare was dead. The theatre had taken a turn toward the escapist in the romances Fletcher wrote with Beaumont, and toward the decadent in the later plays of John Webster (*The Duchess of Malfi* [1613–1614] and *The White Devil* [1612]). But for an audience in need of escapism, John Fletcher wrote a series of attractive and successful works, thriving in his collaborations.

John Fletcher died in the plague of 1625. An engraved stone marking his burial site can be seen between the choir stalls of Southwark Cathedral near the Globe Theatre. Next to him on one side lies the playwright Philip Massinger and on the other is Edmund Shakespeare, William Shakespeare's youngest brother, buried there in 1607.

SHAREHOLDERS AND HOUSEKEEPERS

The Chamberlain's Men
The King's Men
At the Globe and the Blackfriars

Their deserts yet live in the remembrance of many.
An Apology for Actors (1612), Thomas Heywood

Shakespeare's most consistent source of companionship came from his colleagues at work. These were, first, the mixed group of actors who toured the provinces to escape the plague of 1592–1593 under the protection of Lord Strange (sometimes called Derby's Men as Strange was also Lord Derby); and, next, the members of the Lord Chamberlain's Men, a company founded in 1594. Lord Strange had died and the company approached Hunsdon, the Lord Chamberlain, who had sponsored two earlier companies, one from 1564 to 1567 and another from 1581 to 1590. Hunsdon perhaps looked with favor on this request as James Burbage had acted for him in 1584. In any event, it was a happy decision, as this company would be his most distinguished and most famous.

In June 1594, when the actors returned to London from nearly two years of plague-induced exile, the newly founded Lord Chamberlain's Men joined up with the Admiral's Men for ten days at the theatre called Newington Butts, under the management of Philip Henslowe. These performances brought together on the same stage the extraordinary talents of Edward Alleyn and Richard Burbage, the two greatest actors of the day. However, the association was brief; immediately after this booking the companies split and the Admiral's Men stayed with Alleyn and Henslowe to play at the Rose Theatre while the Chamberlain's Men went with James Burbage to his Theatre across the river and up the long road to Shoreditch.

The Chamberlain's Men was set up as a company of actor-shareholders, the first of whom were William Shakespeare, Richard Burbage, John Heminges, Augustine Phillips, William Kempe, Thomas Pope, George Bryan, and Richard Cowley. Under this arrangement (unique for the time) a "sharer," having bought into the company, was both an actor and a part owner of the company's joint stock. As his share of the profits, the shareholder not only got his salary but a portion of the general entrance fees and a portion of the extra fee for gallery seats after expenses for overhead (such as the hiring of extra actors) were deducted. In 1603 Lawrence Fletcher, an actor, joined the group. He had played before the King in Scotland and was a favorite. At this point the Chamberlain's Men became the King's Men, and their number increased to twelve in 1604.

Documentation of the Chamberlain's Men continued in the winter of 1594 when Hunsdon, as their patron, wrote to the lord mayor of London to ask for permission for his company to play at the Cross Keys Inn. On March 15 the next year, Kempe, Burbage, and Shakespeare were listed as payees for two performances of the Lord Chamberlain's Men at Greenwich Palace on December 26 and 27, 1594—the first official record of the company being paid for a performance. This distinguished court engagement was followed the next night, December 28, by the *The Comedy of Errors* at Gray's Inn, where the actors—the finest in London—were described as "a Company of base and common fellows."[28]

In 1596 the city of London forbade any more performances in inns such as the Cross Keys and the company probably went to the Swan Theatre and certainly to the Curtain. The following year the Privy Council limited the licensed London Acting Companies to two: the Admiral's Men and the Lord Chamberlain's Men. Queen Elizabeth commanded twenty performances from the Admiral's Men between 1594 and 1603, and thirty-two from the Chamberlain's Men.

Knowing his lease on the Theatre off Halliwell (Holywell) Street was soon to expire, James Burbage leased a site on the Southbank for a new theatre. The dismantling of the Theatre and the building of the Globe, detailed below in the biographies of Richard and Cuthbert Burbage, was filled with excitement, daring, and risk.

Needing money to construct the Globe, the Burbages created a new syndicate patterned on the shareholder model, which was working well in the company. The two Burbage brothers accepted Will Kempe, Thomas Pope, William Shakespeare, Augustine Phillips, and John Heminges as fellow Globe investors in 1599, making these seven men shareholders (actors) and housekeepers (owners) alike.

Three years earlier James Burbage had bought buildings in the old Blackfriars Priory which had been remodeled into a theatre for the performances of the Children of the Chapel, a boys' acting company.

The property continued as a boys' company venue until 1608 when Richard Burbage took over the lease and formed another new company of housekeepers: himself, his brother Cuthbert, and (familiar names now) Shakespeare, Heminges, Condell, William Sly, and Thomas Evans (probably a relative of the Henry Evans who had held the prior lease). The housekeepers by definition shared ownership of the Blackfriars building and its profits. Though smaller in capacity than the Globe, the Blackfriars was an indoor space that could be used year-round, and as it was more comfortable and elite, a higher price was charged for tickets. As time went by, the revenues from the Blackfriars Theatre far exceeded those of the Globe, and it was from these investments that Shakespeare and his friends became wealthy men.

Within these two groups of housekeepers were Shakespeare's closest associates and, we may assume, some of his best friends: Thomas Pope, Will Kempe, Cuthbert Burbage, Augustine Phillips, Richard Burbage, John Heminges (Globe housekeepers); and Cuthbert and Richard Burbage, John Heminges, William Sly, and an important new addition, Henry Condell (Blackfriars' housekeepers).

Thomas Pope (?–1604)

Why, Hal, 'tis my vocation, Hal, 'tis no sin for a man
to labour in his vocation.

Henry IV, Part 1, act 1, scene 2

Thomas Pope was likely one of the founding members of the Chamberlain's Men in 1594. He was a comedian and an acrobat, which were skills actors possessed in the companies of Shakespeare's time. Along with fellow comedian Will Kempe, he toured to the courts of Denmark and Saxony in 1586 and 1587, and with Lord Strange's Men to the provinces of England in 1593. He was a payee of the Chamberlain's Men with Heminges from 1597 to 1599, and an original housekeeper with the Globe when that syndicate was founded in 1599. From 1598 to 1599 he was in the cast of Ben Jonson's *Every Man in His Humour* and *Every Man Out of His Humour*. Thomas Heywood mentions Pope in his *Apology for Actors*, and Samuel Rowlands refers to the Admiral's comedian John Singer and to Pope in *Letting of Humour's Blood*:

what means Singer then,
And Pope, the clown, to speak so borish, when
They counterfaite the clownes upon the stage?[29]

Thomas Pope and William Kempe were the two clowns in the Chamberlain's Men company, and scholars differ over which one of them might have been the original Falstaff. The role was written when both were shareholders in the company.

Pope lived his whole life in Southwark, made his will in 1603, and died before he could be listed as one of the King's Men.

William Sly (?–1608)

The Slys are no rogues! ... Look in the chronicles,
we came in with Richard Conqueror.
The Taming of the Shrew, act 1, scene 1

His portrait hangs in the Dulwich art collection along with those of several of his colleagues, and Christopher Sly in the Induction to *The Taming of the Shrew* seems to have been written for the actor William Sly. The character shared a name with the performer originating the role, but it was also a common name in the Stratford area, and one assumes the drunken tinker of the play was not a portrait based on the actor. The other role attributed to William Sly by the eminent eighteenth-century scholar Edmond Malone is Osric in *Hamlet*.

Sly belonged at one time to the Admiral's Men: the company owned a costume belonging to him, and in October 1594 Henslowe's diary records that he sold a gold jewel to Sly for eight shillings. However, from 1598 to 1605 Sly is listed as a member of the Chamberlain's/King's Men. As *The Taming of the Shrew* was likely written between 1594 and 1595, it would appear he left the Admiral's Men very shortly after he bought the jewel from Henslowe; or possibly worked for both companies in the mid-1590s. Though not an original Globe housekeeper, Sly became one in 1605.

William Sly lived near the Burbages on Halliwell Street, north of the river in Shoreditch, and was buried in St. Leonard's churchyard. He was friends with Robert Browne, an actor who, unlike the actors having such success in England, made a career for himself on the

Continent. Browne toured Holland, as had Kempe and Pope, then discovered in Germany an eagerness for English plays and performances. He formed the most important English touring company and played in Germany steadily from 1590 to 1607. During his time there in 1593, Browne's entire family died of the London plague.

In 1595, however, Browne married again, a woman named Cecily (possibly Sly's sister) who was the executrix of William Sly's will. Robert Browne was the primary legatee, though Sly also left bequests to Cuthbert Burbage (his sword and his hat) and to James Sands, Augustine Phillips's apprentice, the enormous sum of "fortie pounds." Sly had been an executor and overseer of Phillips's will and had been left a "boule of Silver worth five pounds" when that fellow actor died in 1605.[30] Included in the property Sly left to Robert Browne were his part of the Globe and a recently issued share in the Blackfriars Theatre. Cecily Browne returned the Blackfriars' share to Richard Burbage.

Sly's life contrasted significantly with the family lives that were the norm for the King's Men shareholders. It seems he never married, had a bastard son who was baptized and buried at St. Giles, Cripplegate, and his will was witnessed by several illiterate women.

In 1612 the writer Thomas Heywood wrote his book *Apology for Actors* in answer to increasingly virulent Puritan attacks on the stage. In his book he praises a number of actors, saying:

Here I must remember...Wil Kempe...in the favour of her majesty, as in the opinion and good thoughts of the generall audience. Gabriel, Singer, Pope, Phillips, Sly, all the right I can do them is but this, that, though they be dead, their deserts yet live in the remembrance of many.[31]

Cuthbert Burbage (c. 1566–1636)

Hamlet: Would not this, sir, and a forest of feathers...with two
    provincial roses on my razed shoes, get me a fellowship in a
    cry of players, sir?
Horatio: Half a share.
Hamlet: A whole one, I.

                                  Hamlet, act 3, scene 2

The elder son of James Burbage, Cuthbert was the only non-actor in the group of Globe Theatre and Blackfriars Theatre housekeepers. He had been a servant to Walter Cope, a member of Parliament, who was a close adviser to Lord Burghley and his son Robert Cecil. However, in 1589 Cuthbert's father James asked him to take over the lease of the Theatre on Halliwell (Holywell) Street, and from then on Cuthbert was in the theatre management business.

Cuthbert Burbage took on the job with vigor, daring, and imagination. When his uncle's widow fought with James Burbage for more share in the profits of the theatre than the Burbages felt was owed to her, Cuthbert, along with his father and brother, fought off her assault and were thus summoned for contempt of court.

When Giles Allen refused to renew the lease for the theatre site, Cuthbert, hewing to the letter of the lease, which said the Burbages owned the building if not the land, took action. He organized his friends, company members, and a group of carpenters under the direction of Peter Green and, in a single late-night raid, completely tore down the Theatre. They then moved the parts across the river to the south bank where the theatre was reconstructed as the Globe. This action so infuriated Allen that he left a sputtering, explosive deposition:

Cuthbert Burbage and his followers did "riotously assemble themselves with divers and many unlawful and offensive weapons, as namely, swords, daggers, bills, axes, and such like, and so armed did then repair unto the said Theatre. And then and there, armed as aforesaid, in very riotous, outrageous, and forcible manner, and contrary to the laws of your Highness's realm, attempted to pull down the said Theatre, whereupon divers of your subjects, servants and farmers, then going about in peaceable manner to procure them to disist from that their unlawful enterprise, they, the said riotous persons aforesaid, notwithstanding procured then therein with great violence, not only then and there forcibly and riotously resisting your subjects, servants and farmers, but also then and there pulling, breaking, and throwing down the said Theatre in very outrageous, violent and riotous sort, to the great disturbance and terrifying not only of your subjects, said servants and farmers, but of divers others of your Majesty's loving subjects there near inhabiting."[32]

The reference to farmers indicates how rural the Finsbury Fields area was in the late sixteenth century. The Theatre and the Curtain virtually bordered on fields and farms, making a trip to the theatre also a pleasant walk out to the countryside in those early days.

To finance the rebuilding of the Theatre into the new Globe, Cuthbert Burbage and his younger brother Richard set up a syndicate of investors: they held half the interest in the Globe, then sold the other half of the interest in shares evenly split between Shakespeare, Kempe, Pope, Phillips, and Heminges. One supposes the group of actors was grateful to have in Cuthbert Burbage a member committed to management, not distracted by performance and production.

Burbage married a woman named Elizabeth Cox and had three children: two sons and a daughter. Even after the Globe was built south of the Thames, the Burbages as a family continued to live north on Halliwell (Holywell) Street, Shoreditch, near their father's original theatre.

The business of shareholding worked extremely well for the first generation, as all members of the syndicate were friends directly involved in the business of producing plays. Trouble came as the generation died off and shares were left to others not chosen by the original group. In 1630 John Heminges' son William sold three Globe Theatre shares and two Blackfriars shares, which he had inherited from his father, to actor John Shank (Shank first appears as a King's man in 1619). In 1635 three of the King's Men, Benfield, Pollard, and Swanston, petitioned the Lord Chamberlain Pembroke for the right to buy back the shares. In answer to the Lord Chamberlain's request for information, Cuthbert Burbage wrote:

The father of us Cutbert and Richard Burbage was the first builder of Playhouses and was himselfe in his younger yeares a Player. The Theater hee built with many Hundred poundes taken up at interest. The players that lived in those first times had onely the profitts arising from the dores, but now the players receave all the cummings in at the dores to themselves and halfe the Galleries from the Housekeepers. He built this house upon leased ground, by which meanes the landlord and Hee had a great suite in law, and by his death, the like troubles fell on us, his sonnes; wee then bethought us of altering from thence, and at like expense built the Globe with more summes of money taken up at interest, which lay heavy on us many yeeres and to ourselves wee joined those deserveing men, of that they call the House, but makeing the leases for twenty-one yeeres hathe been the destruction of our selves and others, for they dyeing at the expiration of three or four yeeres of their lease, the subsequent yeeres became dissolved to strangers, as by marrying with their widdowes, and the like by their Children.

Thus, Right Honorable, as concerning the Globe, where wee are but lessees. Now for the Blackfriars that is our inheritance, our father purchased it at extreme rates and made it into a playhouse with great charge and troble, which after was leased out to one Evans that first set up the Boyes commonly called the Queenes Majesties Children of the Chappell. In processe of time the boyes growing up to bee men, which were Underwood, Field, Ostler, and were taken to strengthen the Kings service, and the more to strengthen service, the boyes dayly wearing out, it was considered that house would bee as fitt for our selves, and soe purchased the lease remaining from Evans with our money, and placed men Players, which were Hemings, Condall, Shakspeare, &c.[33]

Cuthbert Burbage outlived almost all of his early contemporaries. He was close to the actors. William Sly, Richard Cowley (who played Verges in *Much Ado About Nothing*), and Nicholas Tooley all left bequests to Cuthbert Burbage in their wills. Sly left him his sword and his hat, while a paragraph in Tooley's will says: "[I] ... do give unto Mrs Burbadge the wife of my good friend Cutbert Burbadge (in whose house I do now lodge) as a remembrance of my love in respect of her motherlie care over me the Some of ten pounds."[34] He is not mentioned in Shakespeare's will, so Shakespeare was not as close to Cuthbert as to his brother Richard. But as a member of the Burbage family and a manager of his company, Shakespeare must have known Cuthbert Burbage very well.

Will Kempe (?–1608)

Where's my knave? My fool? Go you and call my fool hither.
King Lear, act 1, scene 4

Will Kempe's origins are unknown, but his life is documented to a greater degree than most of Shakespeare's actor colleagues because he was a published song writer and author, and in 1590 was reputed to be the "most comical and conceited"[35] actor in England. His book was titled *Kempe's Nine Daies Wonder*, a lively account of a stunt the resourceful Kempe devised to earn money and to keep him in the public eye after he left the Lord Chamberlain's Men in 1599: he would dance a jig every step of the way from London to Norwich. He accomplished the feat between February 11 and March 11, 1600, and wrote about it soon thereafter.

The multitalented Kempe first appears in the early 1580s as a member of the Queen's Men, standing in line to replace the great clown, Richard Tarleton, who was getting on in years. He moved from the Queen's Men to Leicester's Men in the mid-1580s; from 1585 to 1586 he traveled with Leicester to the Low Countries and also went to Denmark before returning to England. Kempe's knowledge of Elsinore is thought by some to have been of interest to Shakespeare in his writing of *Hamlet*.

In 1592 Kempe joined Lord Strange's Men, a company that involved many of Shakespeare's later colleagues and that produced Shakespeare's earliest plays. In 1594 he joined the Lord Chamberlain's Men, the company Shakespeare and his friends formed. For a decade Shakespeare and Kempe worked closely together. Shakespeare's early clown parts were written for Will Kempe, including Peter in *Romeo and Juliet* and Dogberry in *Much Ado About Nothing*. Furthermore, Kempe was one of the original seven shareholders in the Globe Theatre, placing him in the inner circle of Shakespeare's actor friends.

Will Kempe was an actor, a clown, and a song-and-dance man whose job was to provide "merriment." This "merriment" often consisted of wit-cracking improvised repartee at which Kempe excelled. Song-and-dance numbers, often obscene, were also the clown's stock-in-trade. In 1595 the Stationers' Register listed several jigs, one of which was titled "Kempe's New Jigge betwixed a Soldier and A Miser and Sym the Clown." This kind of work was fuel for the Puritans who complained that "Whores, bedles, bawdes and sergeants filthily chaunt Kempe's Jigge."[36]

Shakespeare's friendship with Will Kempe must have been one of the most problematic of his life. Shakespeare was a writer whose plays were crafted with thought and care; any actor who works in them knows the brilliance with which the language of each scene is calculated in its sounds and rhythms to reveal thought, character, relationship, and intention, and—structurally—to pace the play. Kempe's tradition of improvising to an audience eager for his kind of horseplay contributed to the popularity of the Lord Chamberlain's company. But in Hamlet's advice to the players we may hear Shakespeare's own frustrated experience with Will Kempe:

> and let those that play your clowns speak no more than is set down or
> them, for there be of them that will themselves laugh, to set on some
> quantity of barren spectators to laugh too, though in the mean time

some necessary question of the play be then to be considered. (*Hamlet*, act 3, scene 2)

Around the time that Shakespeare was writing this remark, Will Kempe turned his share in the Globe over to the other four actor-shareholders (Shakespeare, Phillips, Pope, and Heminges) and left the company. In a grand show of bravado, he announced his intention to jig all the way from London to Norwich. The mayor of Norwich, perhaps grateful for the publicity the jig brought to his city, gave Kempe an annuity of forty shillings, and Kempe made further money as he solicited contributions and encouraged wagers. An overseer, George Spat, went along to ensure that Kempe danced every step of the way. In his book Kempe wrote that he had "danced himself out of the world," which many interpret as a pun on his leaving the Globe. After he jigged across England, the peripetetic Kempe traveled to Germany and Italy. He came back to be a member of Worcester's Men from 1602 to 1603, and died in 1608.

In contrast to Kempe, there is no evidence that Shakespeare ever travelled out of his corner of England. In fact, a number of lines in Shakespeare's plays express a horror of travel, notably in *As You Like It*, where Rosalind comments on Jacques's melancholy:

> A traveller! By my faith, you have a good reason to be sad....I had rather have a fool to make me merry than experience to make me sad. And to travel for it, too!
>
> *As You Like It*, act 4, scene 1

And Mobray in *Richard II* expresses dread to be away from the English language:

> The language I have learnt these forty years,
> My native English I must now forgo,
> And now my tongue's use is to me no more
> Than an unstringed viol or a harp,
> Or like a cunning instrument, cased up—
> Or being open, put into his hands
> That knows no touch to tune the harmony:
> Within my mouth you have engoaled my tongue,
> Doubly portcullised with my teeth and lips
> And dull, unfeeling barren ignorance
> Is made my goaler to attend on me...

What is thy sentence then but speechless death,
Which robs my tongue from breathing native breath?
... Then thus I turn me from my country's light
To dwell in solemn shades of endless night.

Richard II, act 1, scene 3

In no play of Shakespeare's nor in any of his poetry do we find travel exalted or desired, whereas the love of his native countryside is constantly celebrated.

Shakespearean plays that are set in foreign countries are often faulty in their geography: Illyria (Bohemia) is given a nonexistent coastline in *Twelfth Night*, and the same Bohemia is represented as being both desertlike and having a seacoast in *A Winter's Tale*; in *Two Gentlemen of Verona*, Shakespeare supposes one of the gentlemen can take a ship from Verona or Milan, though neither is near the sea; and in *The Taming of the Shrew*, the Mantuan pedant is going to Rome by way of Padua—a notable detour. None of this is of the least importance—Shakespeare's locales are imaginative, grounded in realism with a familiar place-name here and there. But the mistakes would not have been made by a traveler who had been to the locales.

Will Kempe did not fit into Shakespeare's company. He is the only one of the actor-shareholders who left for any reason other than retirement or death. His place was taken by the new clown Robert Armin, and the style of Shakespeare's writing for clowns became more subtle and lyrical. And there is no further complaint about inappropriate clowning shenanigans. The play had become recognized as the thing.

Augustine Phillips (fl. 1590, d. 1605)

... nought so stockish, hard, and full of rage,
But music for the time doth change his nature.
The man that hath no music in himself
Nor is not moved wih concord of sweet sounds,
Is fit for treasons, stratagems, and spoils.

The Merchant of Venice, act 5, scene 1

On February 7, 1601, Shakespeare's company was hired to play a special performance of his *Richard II* at the Globe. Those asking for the performance were supporters of the Earl of Essex. Ever since September 28, when Essex had returned from his failed expedition to Ireland, great tension had existed between him and the aging Queen Elizabeth. Various political malcontents, chafing under the high-handed decisions of the queen, rallied around Essex, mistakenly persuading him that were he to lead a rebellion against the queen, thousands of citizens would rise up to follow him.

The Chamberlain's men did not want to perform. The play was not in the current repertory, and the Earl of Essex's men specifically requested "the play of the deposyng and kyllyng of Kyng Rychard the second."[37] This play showed the legitimate King Richard deposed by the rebellious Bolingbroke—chancy material in the climate of the time. The Globe was to be the venue, as it would seem the purpose was to hearten the feelings of a large general populace against the queen. The supporters of Essex, one of the most ardent of whom was Shakespeare's old acquaintance the Earl of Southampton, offered the company well above their normal fee and the performance went forward.

The next day Essex and his followers staged their march on the palace. None rose. Essex and Southampton were arrested and imprisoned, and Augustine Phillips was called ten days later to explain to the court the performance of *Richard II*.

> The Examination of Augustyne Phillypps servant unto the L. Chamberlyne and one of hys players taken the xviijth of Februarij 1600 upon his oth.
>
> He sayeth that on Fryday last was sennyght or Thursday Sr Charles Percy, Sr Josclyne Percy and the L. Montegle with some thre more spak to some of the players in the presans of thys examinate to have the play of the deposying and kylling of Kyng Rychard the second to be played the Saturday next promysyng to gete them xls. more than their ordynary to play yt. Wher thys Examinate and hys fellowes were determyned to have played some other play, holdyng that play of Kyng Richard to be so old & so long out of use as that they shold have small or no Company at yt. But at their request this Examinate and his fellowes were Content to play yt the Saterday and had their xls. more than their ordynary for yt and so played yt accordyngly.
>
> Augustine Phillips.[38]

This was as near as Shakespeare ever came to censure for his work.*

Phillips succeeded in convincing the examiners that the acting company had no knowledge of the Essex affair, but given the haste with which writers and actors were often jailed for offending the crown, the company must have breathed a collective sigh of relief when Phillips returned.

The Essex rebellion was on February 8, 1601. On February 18 Phillips gave his testimony about *Richard II*. On the 24th the Chamberlain's Men played before the queen at Whitehall. On the 25th, Essex, once the great favorite of the queen, was executed upon her order.

We have no idea why Augustine Phillips represented the company. His early history—where and when he was born—is equally unknown. We do know that as an adult Augustine Phillips shared a history with Shakespeare, Burbage, Heminges, and Condell, dating back to the early 1590s—in Lord Strange's company of 1591, Phillips is listed in the cast of *Seven Deadly Sins*.

In 1594 Phillips probably joined Burbage to form the Chamberlain's Men. His name appears in the cast lists of Jonson's *Every Man in His Humour*, *Every Man Out of His Humour*, and *Sejanus*. In 1599 he was one of the original Globe housekeepers—that small group of men who were shareholders in the company, in addition to being actor-sharers.

In London he lived in Bankside, but as he, like the other company shareholders in the Globe Theatre, became wealthy and established, he also bought a country house at Mortlake in Surrey. This property became a refuge for the company in times of plague, and they were rehearsing there when called to Lord Pembroke's Wilton House to play for King James.

Phillips was married to a woman named Anne and had five children. He had a particularly close relationship with the Chamberlain's Men, as his sister Elizabeth was married to actor Robert Gough (this couple also became parents to five children). Furthermore, it is thought that his other sister, Margery Borne, might have been the wife of William Borne, an actor with Pembroke's company and later with the Admiral's.

The death of Augustine Phillips in 1605 must have been felt deeply by his friends as well as his family. He remembered his fellow company

* The quarto versions of *Richard II* were printed without the deposition scene, which is evidence of censorship. And Queen Elizabeth, in her Privy Chamber, in the summer following Essex's death, "fell upon the reign of King Richard II, saying, 'I am Richard, know ye not that? ... He that will forget God, will also forget his benefactors; this tragedy was played 40 times in open streets and houses'" (Ian Wilson, 281). But this was a private comment, not a public accusation.

members in his will, both hired men and shareholders. To Heminges and Burbage he left silver bowls and:

> Item I geve and bequeathe unto and amongst the hyred men of the Company which I am of, which shal be at the tyme of my decease, the some of fyve pounds of laufull money of England to be equally distributed amongest them, Item I geve and bequeathe to my Fellowe William Shakespeare a thirty shillings peece in gould, To my Fellowe Henry Condell one other thirty shilling peece in gould, To my Servaunte Christopher Beeston thirty shillings in gould, To my Fellowe Lawrence Fletcher twenty shillings in gould.[39]

Leaving twenty shillings to four other company members, and some of his valuable costume pieces to two of his apprentices, he left to apprentice James Sands "some fortye shillings and a citterne a bandore and a lute."[40]

Phillips's "portion" to his widow Anne was restricted, for she would lose it if she married again. His share in the Globe was contested. The musical instruments left to James Sands indicate that Phillips played an important role as a musician in the King's Men company. His "jig of the slippers" was registered with the Stationers in 1595.

Shakespeare left legacies in his will for only three members of the King's Men: Richard Burbage, John Heminges, and Henry Condell. It is likely that if Phillips had not predeceased him, Shakespeare would have left a similar bequest to his friend Augustine Phillips.

Richard Burbage (c. 1571–1619)

Is it not monstrous that this player here
But in a fiction, in a dream of passion
Could force his soul so to his own conceit
That from her working all his visage wanned,
Tears in his eyes, distraction in his aspect
A broken voice, and his whole function suiting
With forms to his conceit; and all for nothing.
For Hecuba.
What's Hecuba to him, or he to Hecuba
That he should weep for her?

Hamlet, act 2, scene 2

After the retirement of Edward Alleyn in 1605, Richard Burbage was the greatest actor of the early seventeenth century. He was also a painter. In the spring of 1613, the young Earl of Rutland was eager to make a big impression at a tournament held to commemorate the tenth anniversary of King James's accession. In addition to spending a large amount of money on his horse's trappings and on his own plumes and feathers, he paid four pounds and eight shillings to Richard Burbage and William Shakespeare to design a decorative shield for him. All the knights in the tournament had such decorative paper shields (*impresa*) for display, and the competition among them for the best, most intriguing, and most meaningful design was keen. Evidently Shakespeare was to invent the motto and Burbage to paint the shield. As Shakespeare had retired to Stratford by this time, having such a project to lure him back to London must have pleased Burbage. In fact, shortly after this project, Shakespeare bought his only piece of London property: the Blackfriars Gatehouse, a property very near to his company's theatre. It would seem he bought it for investment, as a rental property. However, he might equally have wanted a pied-à-terre in London so that he could easily return to the city from retirement life in Stratford.

Burbage was quite a good painter. An early likeness of him is thought to be a self-portrait, and while the Chandos portrait of Shakespeare that hangs in the National Portrait Gallery was done by an anonymous painter, romantics like to attribute it to Burbage. A portrait of a woman painted by Richard Burbage once hung in Dulwich College, the college founded by his great rival actor Edward Alleyn. So his artistic skills were considerable, and perhaps were used much in the theatre; but his genius was for acting, and his family business was not the art studio, but the theatre.

Shakespeare's relationship with Richard Burbage dated back to his early years in London, when Shakespeare was an aspiring playwright barely twenty-five and Burbage not yet twenty.

James Burbage (1531–1597), Richard's father, was a theatre professional of the robust generation that bridged the gap between late-medieval drama in England and the flowering of great Elizabethan theatre. A leading actor with Leicester's Men, James Burbage built the first English structure designed and used solely for the presentation of plays—the Theatre on Halliwell (variously spelled Holywell) Street, Shoreditch. The Theatre was built in 1576 when he was in his forties and his two sons were very young. A joiner (carpenter) as well as an actor, Burbage and his sons undoubtedly helped in the physical construction of this remarkable building.

The older son of James, Cuthbert Burbage (c. 1567–1636), was not an actor, but spent his life as a theatre manager. As early as 1589 his father nominated him to take over the lease of the Theatre. Cuthbert married Elizabeth Cox and became the father of two sons and a daughter. Throughout Shakespeare's professional life, Cuthbert Burbage was a close colleague.

But as well as Shakespeare knew Cuthbert and his family, and James and his wife Ellen, his closest friend in the family was Richard. They spent a good part of their lives together onstage and backstage. Shakespeare wrote his greatest leading roles specifically for Richard Burbage: Richard III, Hamlet, Macbeth, Othello, King Lear, Prospero, and more.

Richard Burbage was appearing in his father's theatre as early as 1590. We know this because of an incident that had nothing to do with acting. The Theatre was built partly with money from James Burbage's brother-in-law, John Brayne, who was a wealthy grocer. Shortly before his death, Brayne sued Burbage over the distribution of profits, of which Brayne wanted half. When Brayne died, his widow took the suit to Chancery court. She won the case, but when she and her supporters agitated for their money, the Burbages threw them physically and violently out of the Theatre. As a result, James and Cuthbert Burbage were hauled into court for contempt, and the stubborn James did not cease defying the court until the widow died and the action languished. In the altercation Edward Alleyn's brother John (one of the Admiral's Men) reported that he found:

> Ry. Burbage there, with a broome staff in his hand, of whom when his deponente asked what sturre was there he answered in laughing phrase how they came for a moytie. But quod he (holding up the said broomes staff), I haue, I think, deliuered him a moytie with this and sent them packing.[41]

The Burbages did not lie down in the face of adversity. In 1597 the original twenty-one-year lease with Giles Allen, who owned the land on which the Theatre was built, expired. James Burbage had just died and Cuthbert Burbage had inherited the lease. Allen wanted to expel the Burbages from the property and the Theatre. Cuthbert Burbage made efforts to renew the lease, but Allen refused to come to terms. So Cuthbert organized the Chamberlain's Men, and in the dead of night on December 28, 1598, they pulled the entire Theatre down and transported all the reusable timber and building materials across town and across the Thames to Southwark. There they rebuilt the theatre and named it the Globe. The infuriated Allen sued the company, contesting their rights to the building materials. Though the case was in court for four years, it failed when it reached the Star Chamber, where it was opposed by Francis Bacon.

As James Burbage's vision in building a theatre was unique, so the development of the Chamberlain's Men was also innovative: they were the only company of actors to eventually own the theatre building in which they worked. After their former patron, Lord Strange, died in 1594, George Bryan, Richard Cowley, John Heminges, William Kempe, Augustine Phillips, Thomas Pope, Richard Burbage, and William Shakespeare approached Henry Carey, Baron Hunsdon, who was Lord Chamberlain to Queen Elizabeth, to ask for his protection. When he agreed, they became the Lord Chamberlain's Men. In June 1594 they played in the Newington Butts theatre, but they soon moved to the Theatre to become its resident company. When the timbers of the Theatre were moved across the river in 1598, the newly built Globe became their home. The seven major actors in the company plus Cuthbert Burbage thus became the "housekeepers," or management owners.

In 1596 James Burbage bought a second theatre, another innovation, as this was to be an indoor locale. The venue was the Blackfriars, an old Dominican priory held by Sir William More. More had leased the upper space in the building to Richard Farrant, master of the Children of the Chapel, in 1576 so that the boy actors could offer plays to the public. This arrangement ended in 1584. James Burbage bought the buildings from More for 600 pounds and converted the rooms so that there was a hall sixty feet by forty-six feet, with a stage at one end and galleries to the sides—much like the inn yard spaces or the great halls the company often played on tour. However, a group of residents from the Blackfriars district, including the influential Lady Russell and Shakespeare's printer friend Richard Field, complained about the carriages crowding the streets and the upheaval caused by public performances. They succeeded in staving off Burbage's initial plans. As a result, from 1600 to 1608 Richard Burbage leased the space to Henry Evans and Nathaniel Giles for their Children of the Chapel. In 1608 the Blackfriars Theatre started offering performances by the King's Men and the new playing space inspired a change in playwriting style, encouraging masque-like plays, the comedies of Beaumont and Fletcher, and the late romances of Shakespeare.

Richard Burbage, the leading actor of the King's Men, kept his residence on Halliwell Street, in Shoreditch, near the original Theatre. He married a woman named Winifred and had seven or eight children, one named William, and all baptized at St. Leonard's church. Richard and Winifred Burbage also kept at least one apprentice, Nicholas Tooley (the same Tooley who went to live with Cuthbert after Richard Burbage's death and thanked Elizabeth Burbage for her "motherlie care" in his will). For a while Shakespeare lived near the Burbages before he moved to Bankside near the Globe.

After Shakespeare's move the two men still saw each other regularly, rehearsing in the morning and performing in the afternoon. The two roles most consistently and historically attributed to Shakespeare are the ghost in *Hamlet* and old Adam in *As You Like It*. In these plays (and many others) Shakespeare and Burbage acted together, standing close to one another on the stage. We can imagine their thrill the first time emotions found expression in Shakespeare's language and when they explored together, in rehearsal and performance, the complexity of his characters and the subtlety of their relationships. For over twenty years no other writer gave such rich gifts to an actor as Shakespeare gave Burbage; and no other actor of the day was more inspiring to a playwright than Richard Burbage was to William Shakespeare.

All of the actors must have been rewarding to write for, however, for the actors in the Lord Chamberlain's company were the best in an era that produced dozens of performers, all trained to meet the demands of a difficult and competitive craft. First and foremost, Shakespeare and his fellow actors would have had highly trained voices. The demands of the language in the plays were extreme, and people went not to see, but to hear a play. Audibility in a large outdoor space, expressiveness, and the versatility needed to create different characters would be taken for granted and great skill would be very much appreciated. But the actors also had to sing well. When Henry V says, "Let there be sung 'Non Nobis' and 'Te Deum'," fifteen strong male voices would be lifted in harmony and would fill the hall.[42] Singing from a variety of characters and often the whole cast was expected in every play. Dancing was expected as well. In the 1590s a play always ended with a dance—a practice that was used the way we often use a curtain call.

As playwriting developed and changed, this dance ceased to be compulsory. However, the need for actors to dance, move well, and be expert swordsmen and stage-fighters remained. Vocally, physically, and emotionally the actors had to please a critical and demanding audience.

From Hamlet's "Advice to the players," one deduces that, despite the technical demands of the plays' high rhetoric, Shakespeare's company had a taste for believability and realism in their acting style. Burbage as Hamlet would scarcely have had license to utter the following words, if he himself did not provide an example of their practical application:

> Speak the speech, I pray you, as I pronounced it to you trippingly on the tongue, but if you mouth it as many of your players do, I had as lief the town-crier spoke my lines. Nor do not saw the air too much with your hands thus, but use all gently, for in the very torrent, tempest, and as I may say whirlwind of your passion, you must acquire and beget a temperance that may give it smoothness.
>
> (*Hamlet*, act 3, scene 2)

Burbage was described as a "Protean" actor who lived his roles, sustaining his part in speech or silence. His believability is lauded in the elegy on his death:

> Oft have I seen him leap into the grave,
> Suiting the person, that he seemd to have
> Of a young lover, with so true an eye
> That then I would have sworn he meant to die—
> Oft hav I seen him play this part in jest
> So lively that spectators, and the rest
> Of his sad crew, whilst he but seemed to bleed,
> Amazed thought even that he died indeed![43]

Burbage's playing of Richard III produced a personal anecdote recorded by a young lawyer named John Manningham. Manningham kept a diary in which he described a production of *Twelfth Night* performed for the law students at the Middle Temple on February 2, 1602. In that diary he told the story of two of the actors in the Chamberlain's company: Richard Burbage had had such a success in *Richard III* that a "citizen's wife" invited him to an assignation. Shakespeare, it seems, overheard the invitation and got to the lady before

Burbage. Shakespeare and the lady were about their business, when, Manningham tells us, there came a knock at the door. When answer came that Richard III had arrived, Shakespeare sent back word that William the Conqueror came before Richard III.[44] The pat nature of the joke argues against its factual base, but gives us an insight into the high-spirited, joking, witty young men of the time—those who wrote plays and those who watched them. And we hear Richard Burbage answering again "in a laughing phrase."[45]

Burbage and Shakespeare parted company only when Shakespeare went back to Stratford around 1611. By then he and Burbage had worked together for twenty years. He returned to London to design the shield for the Earl of Rutland in 1613; however, the greater lure may have been the chance to work on a project with his old and dear friend Richard Burbage.

In 1616, Shakespeare died at the age of 52, leaving Burbage money for a memorial ring. Three years later, Burbage died close to the same age. Compared to Shakespeare, Heminges, and Condell, Burbage's estate was small, but his legacy was enormous. All London mourned. An elegy on the death of Burbage expressed the city's grief:

> He's gone, and with him what a world is dead!
> Which he revived, to be revived so
> No more! Young Hamlet, ould Heironymoe,
> Kind Leer, the greued Moore, and more beside
> That lived in him, haue now for ever dy'de.[46]

Queen Anne died the same year, in the same month—March. The playwright Middleton wondered that there was so little grief for the queen's passing and so much for Burbage:

> When he expires, lo! all lament that man,
> But where's the grief should follow good Queen Anne?[47]

Two months later the Earl of Pembroke could not bear to go to the theatre, even to see a special presentation for the French ambassador. He did not want to see a play so soon after the death of his "old acquaintance Burbage."[48]

Ultimately, the most moving remark on the death of Burbage was the most terse—two simple words:

> Exit Burbage.[49]

John Heminges (c. 1556–1630)

Then fear not, Burbage, heaven's angry rod,
When thy fellows are angels and old Heminges is God.
Anonymous poem on the death of Richard Burbage

John Heminges' birth date is unknown, but he was older than Richard Burbage, Henry Condell, and William Shakespeare; yet by 1630 when he died, he had outlived all these old friends of the King's Men. His father, from Droitwich, England, came from a Worcestershire family, but virtually all of John Heminges' life was spent in London, and most of that in St. Mary's Parish, Aldermanbury, where he lived near his friend Henry Condell.

In 1588 Heminges married Rebecca Knell, who had been widowed the year before. Her husband, William Knell, an actor with the queen's company, assaulted a fellow actor and was killed by him while the company was on tour at Thame in Oxfordshire. Several months later the Queen's Men played Stratford, fueling speculation that Shakespeare might have joined the company at that time to take Knell's place and left with them for London.

John and Rebecca Heminges had fourteen children, four of whom predeceased them. One daughter left intriguing details about her father. That daughter, Thomasine, married a young actor in the King's Men company, William Ostler, who unfortunately died intestate while still in his twenties. Heminges claimed Ostler's shares in the Globe and Blackfriars Theatres, and Thomasine took her father to court in order to recover them. She and her father reconciled, but Heminges did not follow through with what she felt he owed her, and she sued him again, this time for 600 pounds in damages. It seems Heminges kept the shares, which he eventually passed on to his son William, a playwright.

In 1593 Heminges belonged to Lord Strange's Men and toured the provinces with Edward Alleyn. In all likelihood Heminges joined Burbage and the others when the Chamberlain's Men was founded the next year. Once he joined the company, he remained with them his entire professional life.

Heminges was a character actor suited to roles like Polonius in *Hamlet*, Duke Senior in *As You Like It*, and Egeus in *A Midsummer Night's Dream*. When the Globe thatch caught fire in 1613, and the

theatre burned to the ground, an anonymous balladeer recording the
catastrophe wrote:

> Then with swolne eyes, like druncken Flemminges,
> Distressed stood old stuttering Heminges.[50]

It seems he had already stopped acting by then, however, as
the last play recording an appearance by Heminges was *Catiline* in
1611.

Every one of the King's Men housekeepers had responsibilities
toward the company in addition to acting. Shakespeare's responsi-
bility was writing plays. Heminges' was business management and—
according to a fine bit of sleuthing by Ian Wilson—concessions. In
Shakespeare, The Evidence, Ian Wilson points out that Heminges was
described in his will as a grocer. In fact he became a full member of the
Worshipful Company of Grocers in 1595, the year after the Chamberlain's Men had formed. In Philip Henslowe's diary, a very carefully
made agreement was noted for an exclusive arrangement with John
Cholmley to provide food and drink in the environs of the Rose
Theatre. Surely an analogous arrangement was handled by Heminges
at the Globe. Doubtless he put his children to work selling nuts, ap-
ples, oranges, gingerbread, and beer at the theatre—food he was able
to get wholesale through his grocer's license. By 1621 Heminges was
admitted to the Grocer's Livery, which meant he superintended fancy
banquets for aristocratic guests. Concessions and catering undoubtedly helped build his fortune.

In addition to helping manage the King's Men, Heminges advised a
number of the actors on their wills, and Shakespeare asked him to be a
trustee when he bought the Blackfriars Gatehouse in 1613. Like the
other housekeepers, Heminges amassed a considerable fortune. At his
death he owned a quarter of the shares in the Globe and the Blackfriars. He was buried in the church of St. Mary, Aldermanbury, where
the garden holds a statue of Shakespeare and a monument to his two
friends, John Heminges and Henry Condell.

John Heminges was an actor, a grocer, and a theatre manager. But
as a friend of William Shakespeare, Heminges' most significant
contribution was achieved in collaboration with his friend Henry
Condell: the issuing of the First Folio of William Shakespeare's plays,
an achievement of such monumental importance it is discussed sep-
arately, in its own chapter.

Henry Condell (c. 1562–1627)

I have gone here and there
And made myself a motley to the view.
                    Sonnet #110, William Shakespeare

It is thought that Henry Condell started life as an actor by being an apprentice to John Heminges. It is possible Condell entered the Chamberlain's Men company when it was founded in 1594, but it is certain that in 1598 he was a shareholder; by 1603 he had a share and was a housekeeper in the Blackfriars Theatre, and by 1612 in the Globe as well.

T. W. Baldwin identifies Henry Condell's line as an actor as the "distinguished young man," but he was versatile enough to play both comedic and tragic parts (the Cardinal in Webster's *Duchess of Malfi* and various roles in Jonson's comedies). In *They Gave Us Shakespeare*, Charles Connell envisions Condell playing Antony to Heminges' Caesar (*Julius Caesar*), Malcolm to his Ross (*Macbeth*), Edgar to his Kent (*King Lear*), and Horatio to his Polonius (*Hamlet*).

Condell married a very wealthy woman who owned a great deal of property. They had nine children. Condell lived most of his life near John Heminges—they were both churchwardens at St. Mary, Aldermanbury, and both are buried there.

A popular man among his fellow actors and shareholders, toward the end of his life Henry Condell entertained his colleagues at the country estate to which he had retired. He was left bequests in the wills of Augustine Phillips, Alexander Cooke (who named Condell the trustee for his four children), Nicholas Tooley (who called Condell his loving friend), John Underwood, and William Shakespeare.

The high standing of the King's Men is confirmed when we read that both Heminges and Condell were granted royal allowances for black cloth to make outfits for King James' funeral procession in 1625.

When Shakespeare died in 1616, he left Heminges and Condell each twenty-six shillings and eight pence. He granted them this money (as he had his third dear actor friend, Richard Burbage) to purchase memorial rings. Wealthier even than Shakespeare, Henry Condell died at his Fulham estate in 1627, four years after helping John Heminges publish the First Folio of Shakespeare's plays.

THE WIVES

You are sad. Get thee a wife! Get thee a wife!
Much Ado About Nothing, act 5, scene 4

In Stratford:
Judith Sadler
Bess Quiney
Anne Digges Russell
Ann Shaw Aspinall

Our own experience teaches that when we have long-established friendships with friends who live near us, the likelihood is great that we will develop bonds of friendship with their spouses as well.

In Stratford the youthful Shakespeare certainly knew Judith Sadler almost as well as his friend Hamnet Sadler. And if he first knew Bess Quiney through his friend Richard, she undoubtedly became an even closer friend after Richard Quiney died: she lived near Anne Shakespeare while she finished raising her nine children, and became part of the Shakespeare family when their youngest daughter Judith married her son Thomas.

Anne Digges Russell first lived near Shakespeare in London and was a friend to him, John Heminges, and Henry Condell before marrying Thomas Russell. They moved from London to Rushock Manor, Droitwich, near Stratford and remained close enough friends that Thomas Russell was one of the overseers of Shakespeare's will.

Ann Shaw was the mother of Julius (July) Shaw, the high bailiff of Stratford who witnessed Shakespeare's will, and the wife of Alexander Aspinall. She had inherited a wool business from her first husband, which gave Aspinall his opportunity to thrive as a businessman as well as an academic. As the Shaws were neighbors of the Shakespeares on Henley Street, Ann Shaw Aspinall was known to Shakespeare through both her marriages.

In London:
Jacqueline Vautrollier Field

Rebecca Heminges
Elizabeth Condell
Winifred Burbage

In London, the course of events in Jacqueline Vautrollier's life represent a not-uncommon pattern of the time period: the wife of the master, upon his death, becomes the wife of the apprentice (though in this case there is question whether the Jacqueline whom Richard Field married was Vautrollier's wife or his daughter). Whichever Jacqueline he married, the wedding brought Richard Field the business and, with his wife, Field made a great success of it. Jacqueline Field was a French Huguenot refugee, and when Richard's young friend from Stratford, William Shakespeare, needed help with the French language for the characters in his early plays, she was a ready source of information for the novice playwright.

Later, a quarter century of close friendship with John Heminges, Henry Condell, and Richard Burbage surely included a friendship with their wives. Shakespeare lived within a short walk of the Hemingeses and the Condells and visiting their lively, busy homes, filled with babies, growing children, and apprentices, must have given Shakespeare a break from the loneliness of his rented lodgings.

Rebecca Heminges had a lifetime of connection with the theatre. Before marrying John Heminges she had been the young wife of the actor William Knell. While on tour with the Queen's Company he was killed in an assault by a fellow actor. A few months later Rebecca remarried; her new husband was another actor, the young John Heminges. Their marriage took place in 1588, just about the time William Shakespeare arrived in London from Stratford. A testimony to the Hemingeses' happy marriage is the desire expressed by John Heminges in his will that he be buried near his beloved wife.

The Hemingeses had fourteen children, and John Heminges sustained two careers—one in the theatre and the other as a wholesale grocer. It is altogether likely that while John saw to his work in the theatre, Rebecca managed the grocery business. Ian Wilson suggests that the Hemingeses' commitment to the grocery business may have been a means of getting wholesale foods—nuts, oranges and so forth—to sell as concessions at the Globe Theatre. It is easy to imagine this as a family business, with fourteen children to draw upon as concessionaires over decades of play production.

From 1596 on, Rebecca Heminges' near neighbor was Elizabeth Condell, wife of Henry Condell. Elizabeth came from a far different background than Rebecca Heminges: a wealthy heiress, Elizabeth Condell owned twelve houses in the Strand which she brought to her marriage.

The Condells had nine children as compared to the Heminges' fourteen and the Burbages' eight. Elizabeth and Henry managed their money well, and at the end of their lives, Henry Condell retired (far richer than Shakespeare), to an estate he and his wife had bought in Fulham.

The Burbage family lived to the northwest, outside the city gates near the Theatre built by the patriarch James Burbage in 1576. Shakespeare would not have found it so easy to stop by for a visit.

After Richard Burbage died in 1619, his widow Winifred remarried another actor in the King's Men company, Richard Robinson. She lived until after 1635, when she was listed along with her son William in the Sharer's Petition (Halliday, *A Shakespeare Companion*).

As they led private not public lives, these women friends of Shakespeare flew under Elizabethan radar, so less is known of them than of their husbands. Nonetheless, when we look at them as a group, an interesting picture emerges. They often combined life as mothers and homemakers with working life, as women do today. In Stratford, Judith Staunton Sadler bore fourteen children, half of whom died. A bakery such as the Sadlers' was likely to be a family business, absorbing whatever help Judith could contribute as well as requiring the help of the children as they grew.

Another hardworking woman was Bess Quiney, who inherited and ran a tavern in Stratford after the death of her husband left her with nine children to support.

Anne Digges Russell was more fortunate. She and her husband were wealthy, and she had no need to work. However, she had fought a long and difficult battle to break the provision in her husband's will that stipulated she would lose her inheritance from him if she re-married. Her battle on this issue with her oldest son Dudley tore the family apart. She had the courage to live openly with Thomas Russell until she won her case and was able to marry him.

Anne Digges would have been one of the more intellectual of Shakespeare's women friends. Her first husband was a member of Parliament, a writer, a scientist, and one of the most brilliant orators of his day. Dudley followed in his father's footsteps, while Anne's second son Leonard was an Oxford scholar and linguist who wrote an encomium to Shakespeare for the publication of the First Folio, thus confirming the close friendship of the Digges/Russell family with Shakespeare.

The rich and varied portraits of women Shakespeare gives us in his plays are the product of his imaginative genius. It is impossible to point to one character and say that he or she was based on one particular friend. However, the wide variety of women Shakespeare knew and counted as his friends are the reality mirrored by the plays, and our enjoyment of Rosalind and Viola, Portia and Beatrice, Mistress Page and Mistress Ford, is enhanced when we join to them visions of Anne Digges and Jacqueline Field, Judith Sadler and Bess Quiney, Rebecca Heminges and Elizabeth Condell, the wives of his dear friends.

The First Folio (1623)

✦ ✦

To yow that jointly with undaunted paynes
Vowtsafed to chawnte to us thease noble straynes
How much you merrytt by it is not sedd
But you have bleased the living loved the dead.

                    From a seventeenth-century commonplace book,
                                        The Salusbury Family

In 1623 John Heminges and Henry Condell, in a generous act of friendship, gave the world eighteen of Shakespeare's plays and guaranteed that the other eighteen (which had appeared in quartos of various quality) would be read and known as their author intended. Among the lost plays would have been: *Julius Caesar*; *As You Like It*; *Twelfth Night*; *All's Well That Ends Well*; *Measure for Measure*; *Macbeth*; *Antony and Cleopatra*; *Coriolanus*; *Henry VIII*; *Henry VI, Part I*; *The Two Gentlemen of Verona*; *Comedy of Errors*; *The Taming of the Shrew*; *King John*; *Timon of Athens*; *Cymbeline*; *The Winter's Tale*; and *The Tempest*.

Jaggard, a London publisher, issued a faulty collection (now called the "False Folio") in 1619 that was so incomplete and filled with errors that it may have persuaded Heminges and Condell of the necessity of taking control of the project. In any event, they negotiated with Jaggard for an official publication. Looking at the list of lost plays, we can see that the world's debt to the vision and persistence of these two friends of Shakespeare is incalculable.

Theirs was not an easy job. As members of the King's Men and housekeepers of the Globe and Blackfriars Theatres, they would have known where the prompt copies of Shakespeare's plays were kept. And they might have had the editorial help of Edward Knight, the King's Men's bookkeeper. But collecting all of them, freeing those from copyright that had been listed with the Stationer's Register and published in quarto form, editing each script, and working with the printer to prepare them for publication took them three years.

To ensure the book's success, they asked renowned poets to write commendatory verses (Ben Jonson's were quoted earlier) and they made certain the book had distinguished patrons. Heminges and Condell dedicated the book to the two sons of the Pembroke family:

> To the most Noble and Incomparable Pair of Brethren. William Earl of Pembroke, &c. Lord Chamberlain to the King's Most Excellent Majesty. And Philip, Earl of Montgomery, &c. Gentleman of his Majesty's Bedchamber. Both Knights of the most noble Order of the Garter, and our singular good Lords.

They acknowledge the lords' former patronage and their own trepidation in such a dedication, but refer to the esteem both men felt for Shakespeare's work:

> Whilst we study to be thankful in our particular for the many favors we have received from your Lordships, we are fallen upon the ill fortune, to mingle two the most diverse things that can be, fear, and rashness; rashness in the enterprise, and fear of the success. For, when we value the places your Highnesses sustain, we cannot but know their dignity greater, than to descend to the reading of these trifles: and while we name them trifles, we have deprived ourselves of the defence of our Dedication. But since your Lordships have been pleased to think these trifles something, heretofore; and have prosecuted both them, and their Author living, with so much favor, we hope (that they outliving him, and he not having the fate, common with some, to be the executor to his own writings) you will use the like indulgence toward them, you have done unto their parent. There is a great difference, whether any book choose his patrons, or find them: this hath done both. For, so

much were your Lordship's likings of the several parts, when they were acted, as before they were published, the volume asked to be yours.

Heminges and Condell diminish their own role in the publication of the book, revealing as they do so a touching love and loyalty to their dead friend:

> We have but collected them, and done an office to the dead, to procure his orphans, guardians; without ambition either of self-profit, or fame: only to keep the memory of so worthy a friend, and fellow alive, as was our SHAKESPEARE, by humble offer of his plays, to your most noble patronage.

They apologize for their inability to make the book worthy of its patrons, comparing their gift to the offerings of tenant farmers to their squire/lords, or foreigners when approaching their gods; they flatter the lords by acknowledging that gifts become precious, if not by their own merits, then by the nature of the recipients':

> Wherein, as we have justly observed, no man to come near your Lordships but with a kind of religious address, it hath been the height of our care, who are the presenters, to make the present worthy of your Highnesses by the perfection. But there we must also crave our abilities to be considered, my lords. We cannot go beyond our own powers. Country hands reach forth milk, cream, fruits, or what they have; and many nations (we have heard) that had not gums and insense, obtained their requests with a leavened cake. It was no fault to approach their gods, by what means they could; and the most, though meanest, of things are made more precious, when they are dedicated to temples.

It is in this spirit that Heminges and Condell offer the First Folio of Shakespeare's plays to the Pembroke brothers.

> In that name, therefore, we most humbly consecrate to your Highnesses these remains of your servant SHAKESPEARE; that what delight is in them, may be ever your Lordships', the reputation his, and the faults ours, if any be committed, by a pair so careful to show their gratitude both to the living, and the dead, as is
>
> Your Lordships' most bounden,
John Heminges
Henry Condell[1]

Heminges and Condell wrote a second dedication, "To The Great Variety of Readers," which includes us. First, they want all of us to buy the book:

> From the most able, to him that can but spell; there you are numbered. We had rather you were weighed. Especially, when the fate of all books depends upon your capacities: and not of your heads alone, but of your purses. Well, it is now public, and you will stand for your privileges, we know: to read, and censure. Do so, but buy it first. That doth best commend a book, the stationer says. Then, how odd soever your brains be, or your wisdoms, make your licence the same, and spare not. Judge your sixpen'orth, your shilling's worth, your five shillings' worth at the same time, or higher, so you rise to the just rates, and welcome. But, whatever you do, buy. Censure will not drive a trade, or make the jack go.

Heminges and Condell state that they are open to criticism. But these plays are not likely to be harshly judged because they have already been proven successes in the theatre.

> And though you be a magistrate of wit, and sit on the stage at Blackfriars, or the Cockpit, to arraign plays daily, know, these plays have had their trial already, and stood out all appeals; and do now come forth quitted rather by a decree of court, than any purchased letters of commendation.

They lament that Shakespeare did not live long enough to supervise the publication of his work, and apologize for their own inadequacies.

> It had been a thing, we confess, worthy to have been wished, that the Author himself had lived to have set forth and overseen his own writings; but since it hath been ordained otherwise, and he by death departed from that right, we pray you do not envy his friends the office of their care, and pain, to have collected and published them;

Heminges and Condell admit that they are proud they have substituted carefully edited copies of the plays to replace the corrupt quartos formerly published:

> and so to have published them, as where (before) you were abused with divers stolen, and surreptitious copies, maimed, and deformed by the

frauds and stealths of injurious impostors, that exposed them; even those, are now offered to your view cured, and perfect of their limbs, and all the rest, absolute in their numbers, as he conceived them.

"Absolute in their numbers" suggests that they felt *Pericles* was not clearly enough Shakespeare's own work to be included. As in *Two Noble Kinsmen*, Shakespeare had a hand in *Pericles*, but Heminges and Condell included neither work in this collection and offer no excuse. We can only assume that that these plays were not Shakespeare's own. *Troilus and Cressida* is missing, according to Robert Payne, because the manuscript was located when the First Folio was already at the press.[2] They go on to praise the talent and skill of Shakespeare:

Who, as he was a happy imitator of Nature, was a most gentle expresser of it. His mind and hand went together; and what he thought, he uttered with that easiness, that we have scarce received from him a blot in his papers.

But the real praise must come not from them, but from the reader:

But it is not our province, who only gather his works, and give them to you, to praise him. It is yours that read him. And there we hope, to your divers capacities, you will find enough, both to draw and hold you; for his wit can no more lie hid, than it could be lost.

Then follows their most important advice:

Read him, therefore; and again, and again: and if then you do not like him, surely you are in some manifest danger not to understand him.

And their ultimate trust:

And so we leave you to other of his friends, who, if you need, can be your guides: if you need them not, you can lead yourselves, and others. And such readers we wish him.

John Heminges
Henry Condell[3]

In 1622, the year before the First Folio was published, the King's Men, led by John Heminges and Henry Condell, made their one and only visit to Stratford. Shakespeare had died six years before. Perhaps they wanted to see his final resting place. Perhaps they wanted to pay their respects to his widow and daughters. They were all aware that, for the first time, members of Shakespeare's family and his friends who had never come to London would have the chance to see one of his plays performed by his company. This visit then was a time to unify the two parts of William Shakespeare's life: the friends of his successful London career could meet those of his beloved rural origins to celebrate his achievements. When they arrived in Stratford the leaders of the company, Shakespeare's colleagues went, as was customary, to the bailiff to request a license to perform.

But twice, once in 1602 and again in 1611 (the year Shakespeare moved back to Stratford), the increasingly Puritanical town government had passed a resolution forbidding plays to be performed in the town hall.

Hidden insignificantly in the middle of the chamberlain's accounts for the year 1622 is the entry that reveals how difficult it must have been for Shakespeare to reconcile his two lives and his very separate groups of friends, for the entry coldly says:

Payd to the king's players for not playing in the hall, 6 shillings.

Conclusion

✦ ✦

I like to think how Shakespeare pruned his rose
And ate his pippin in his orchard close.
William Rose Benet (1886–1950)

The biographies of Shakespeare's friends reveal much about Shakespeare himself. His London friends were diverse, cutting across lines of class and gender. His mature Stratford friends, however, mirrored the traits he cultivated in himself; they were intelligent, practical, wealthy, successful, upper-middle-class gentry. But even they crossed lines of religious belief: he had friends who were Catholic sympathizers and friends who were deeply Protestant. Professionally, many of them were lawyers, but intellect alone did not attract him. Only Alexander Aspinall, not a particularly close friend, was an intellectual. However, Aspinall was not just a university-educated pedagogue, but a gifted man of business and an active city councilman as well.

The friends from London whom Shakespeare remembered in his will were conservative, family-oriented, actor-managers from his company: John Heminges, Henry Condell, and Richard Burbage. The friendships he sustained with them are worth remark. The Chamberlain's

Men, which became the King's Men, involved a business relationship that endured for over two decades. The membership in this company was unusually stable. Of the early partners, only Will Kempe left after the first five years. The membership afterward changed only with the death of individual actors, or the promotion of apprentices whom the actors and actor-managers had trained in their homes. The aging of the company is reflected in Shakespeare's later plays, where a predominant number of male roles (*King Lear*, *The Tempest*, *The Winter's Tale*, *Cymbeline*, *Henry VIII*) have been written for older rather than younger men. The ability to cooperate and work together over such a long period argues an evenness of temperament and a capacity for understanding among Shakespeare, Heminges, Condell, and the Burbages that must be regarded as remarkable.

Compared to many of his playwright acquaintances, Shakespeare lived a long and peaceful life: Marlowe died in a tavern brawl at the age of twenty-nine; Greene, of dissipation at thirty-four; Kyd, after imprisonment, at thirty-five. Longtime survivor Ben Jonson was known for his contentious, volatile spirit. A constant brawler, Jonson killed a man in a fight, was imprisoned twice, dove into Roman Catholicism for twelve years despite the political risks, pilloried his writing colleagues, complained about Shakespeare's facility, and argued passionately about playwriting theory.

In contrast, except for Robert Greene, who out of jealousy called Shakespeare an "upstart crow," all those who wrote of Shakespeare used the same epithets to describe him: sweet Shakespeare; sweet swan of Avon; honey-tongued, gentle Shakespeare.

He was resolutely private. In an age of public service, when citizens of an English town or city were expected to serve on town councils, and when his friends Heminges and Condell were both wardens of their church, Shakespeare shunned public life and service. In a convivial time, when groups were organized to gather regularly at places like the Mermaid Tavern, Shakespeare chose to be a casual visitor, an outsider.

He kept no personal or business correspondence, and made no effort to publish his plays. The only publications he sought were for his two epic poems *Venus and Adonis* and *The Rape of Lucrece*, when he was a young man less than thirty years old. Perhaps the attention and fame they brought discomfited him. The publication of his *Sonnets* in 1609 was done without his permission and was instantly suppressed. All of this creates the impression of an introverted personality, chary of his privacy.

He was concerned and careful about money. Perhaps haunted into his adulthood by the failure of his father's business, Shakespeare the son invested his money wisely in real estate and tithes in Stratford, and shortly before he died purchased a property in London.

Though litigation was the way of settling small disputes at the time, the lawsuits involving Shakespeare mostly dealt with simple matters of taxes, unpaid debts, and titles to land. They were few in number for the time, and were easily settled. The position he took in the Mountjoy lawsuit, where he was called upon to make a deposition concerning the financial settlement the Mountjoys had made at the time of their daughter's marriage, showed him cautious and unwilling to become involved any more than necessary. He simply said he did not remember the financial details.

Shakespeare was ambitious for distinction; the achievement of a coat of arms in his father's name was important to him, and the motto "Not Without Right" says a great deal about the pride that was wounded with his father's financial ruin. He wanted, and purchased, a fine house in which to live, in Stratford, and a variety of other properties in his home county. Though his circle of friends in Stratford was distinguished and extensive, it seems he could not cut his ties to London. The purchase of the Blackfriars Gatehouse in 1613, the only property he ever bought in London, indicates his need for a connection to his business and friends there even after his retirement.

On a warmer, more personal side, he seems to have valued children, leaving several of them bequests in his will, giving young Robert Davenant the memory of Shakespeare covering him with kisses on a visit to the family's inn in Oxford, becoming a godparent upon request, and writing children's parts with great sensitivity in a number of his plays.

The anecdotes that persist, attributing to him the dalliance with the pretty woman (where he declared to Richard Burbage that William the Conqueror came before Richard III), the epitaph for John Combe, the rhyme for the gloves from Alexander Aspinall and—more to the point—the gaiety of much of the comedy in his work, argue the capacity for sparkling quick wit, light spirits, and high good humor.

In *Richard II*, King Richard tries to persuade his followers that he, a king, is a man as they are, and he cries out from his heart that he needs friends. Businesslike, private Shakespeare lived much of his life in rented lodgings, alone in London, two or three days' distance from his wife and his children. A good part of the year he was traveling from one town to the next across rural England. He was a man who needed friends. And we get a glimpse of him through the friends he valued in his own life. Because he honored friendship by writing of it so eloquently, Shakespeare gives us characters who are friends (to each other and to us), a vocabulary to celebrate our own friendships, and more—for through these gifts we feel that he, too, becomes our friend.

Appendix A

Friendship in Shakespeare's Plays

✦— ⸺✦

Shakespeare presents an astonishing variety of friendships in his plays.

Friendships between men:

Hamlet and Horatio	*Hamlet*
Brutus and Cassius	*Julius Caesar*
Petruchio and Hortensio	*The Taming of the Shrew*
Sir Toby Belch and Andrew Aguecheek	*Twelfth Night*
Iago and Othello	*Othello*
Iago and Roderigo	*Othello*
Polixenes and Leontes	*The Winter's Tale*

Friendships between women:

Celia and Rosalind	*As You Like It*
Helena and Hermia	*A Midsummer Night's Dream*
Mistress Quickly and Doll Tearsheet	*Henry IV, Parts 1* and *2*
Desdemona and Emilia	*Othello*

Portia and Nerissa	*The Merchant of Venice*
Mistress Page and Mistress Ford	*The Merry Wives of Windsor*
Paulina and Hermione	*The Winter's Tale*

Friendships (perhaps surprisingly) between men and women:

Falstaff and Mistress Quickly	*Henry IV, Parts 1* and *2*
Pistol, Bardolph, and Mistress Quickly	*Henry IV* and *Henry V*
Sir Toby Belch and Maria	*Twelfth Night*
Kent and Cordelia	*King Lear*

Friendships between old people:

| Justice Shallow and Silence | *Henry IV, Part 2* |
| Falstaff and Doll Tearsheet | *Henry IV, Part 2* |

Friendships between young people:

| Proteus and Valentine | *Two Gentlemen of Verona* |
| Romeo, Mercutio, et al. | *Romeo and Juliet* |

Friendships between old and young:

| Corin and Silvius | *As You Like It* |
| The Countess and Helen | *All's Well That Ends Well* |

Friendships between servant and master:

Orlando and Adam	*As You Like It*
The Nurse and Juliet	*Romeo and Juliet*
Julia and Lucetta	*Two Gentlemen of Verona*
Kent and Lear	*King Lear*
Oberon and Puck	*A Midsummer Night's Dream*
Pisanio and Imogen	*Cymbeline*

Friendships between relatives:

Adriana and Luciana	*A Comedy of Errors*
The Dromio brothers	*A Comedy of Errors*
Beatrice and Hero	*Much Ado About Nothing*

Friendships between spouses:

Lady Macbeth and Macbeth	*Macbeth*
Hotspur and Kate	*Henry IV, Part 1*
The Duke and Duchess of York	*Richard II*

Friendships between high-born and low-born:

Antonio and Sebastian	*Twelfth Night*
The Captain and Viola	*Twelfth Night*
Sir Toby and Feste	*Twelfth Night*

Friendships between the like-minded:

Duke Senior and his forest friends	*As You Like It*
The King of Navarre and his Lords	*Love's Labours Lost*
The Princess of France and her Ladies	*Love's Labours Lost*

Friendships between opposites:

Don Armado and Moth	*Love's Labours Lost*
Jacques and Duke Senior	*As You Like It*
King Lear and the Fool	*King Lear*

Within plays, people who are friends often talk about friendship:

The Winter's Tale, 1.2:

> Hermione
> You were pretty lordlings then?

Polixenes
We were, fair queen,
Two lads, that thought there was no more behind,
But such a day tomorrow, as to-day,
And to be boy eternal....
We were as twinned lambs that did frisk i' th' sun,
And bleat the one at th'other: what we changed
Was innocence for innocence; we knew not
The doctrine of ill-doing, nor dreamed
That any did.

A Midsummer Night's Dream, 3.2:

Helena
Injurious Hermia, most ungrateful maid,
Have you conspired, have you with these contrived
To bait me with this foul derision?
Is all the counsel that we two have shared,
The sisters' vows, the hours that we have spent
When we have chid the hasty-footed time
For parting us—O! is all forgot?
All school-days' friendship, childhood innocence?
We, Hermia, like two artificial gods,
Have with our needles created both one flower
Both on one sampler, sitting on one cushion,
Both warbling of one song, both in one key;
As if our hands, our sides, voices, and minds,
Had been incorporate. So we grew together,
Like to a double cherry, seeming parted,
But yet an union in partition,
Two lovely berries moulded on one stem:
So with two seeming bodies, but one heart,
Two of the first, like coats in heraldry,
Due but to one, and crowned with one crest.
And will you rend our ancient love asunder
To join with men in scorning your poor friend?
It is not friendly, 'tis not maidenly—

As You Like It, 1.3:

>   Celia
> Shall we be sundred? Shall we part, sweet girl?
> No, let my father seek another heir...
> Therefore devise with me how we may fly
> Whither to go and what to bear with us,
> And do not seek to take your change upon you,
> To bear your griefs yourself and leave me out
> For, by this heaven, now at our sorrow's pale
> Say what thou canst, I'll go along with thee.

As You Like It, 2.7:

>   Orlando
> Then but forbear your food a little while,
> Whiles like a doe I go to find my fawn
> And give it food. There is an old poor man,
> Who after me hath many a weary step
> Limped in pure love: till he be first sufficed
> Oppressed with two weak evils, age and hunger,
> I will not touch a bit.

The Merchant of Venice, 3.2:

>   Portia
> There are some shrewd contents in yon same paper
> That steals the colour from Bassanio's cheek—
> Some dear friend dead, else nothing in the world
> Could turn so much the constitution
> Of any constant man...

>   Bassanio
> The dearest friend to me, the kindest man,
> The best conditioned and unwearied spirit
> In doing courtesies: and one in whom
> The ancient Roman honour more appears
> Than any that draws breath in Italy.

Hamlet, 1.3:

Polonius
Be thou familiar but by no means vulgar.
Those friends thou hast, and their adoption tried,
Grapple them unto thy soul with hoops of steel...

Macbeth, 5.3:

Macbeth
...that which would accompany old age,
As honor, love, obedience, troops of friends,
I must not look to have.

What Shakespeare's Contemporaries Said about Him

╪═ ═╪

Robert Greene, *Greene's Groats-worth of Witte, bought with a Million of Repentance* (1592; pamphlet; in Halliday, *A Shakespeare Companion*, 196)

Greene, a university wit, disparages Shakespeare in this thinly disguised attack.

> Yet trust them not; for there is an upstart Crow, beautified with our feathers, that with his "Tyger's heart wrapped in a player's hide" supposes he is as well able to bombast out a blank verse as the best of you: and being an absolute "Johannes factotum" is in his own conceit the only Shakescene in a country.

Thomas Nashe, *Pierce Peniless* (1593; satire; in Schoenbaum, 153)

Defending himself from the accusation that he had authored Greene's pamphlet, Nashe calls it a "scald, trivial, lying pamphlet."

Henry Chettle, *Kind-Hart's Dreame* (1592; pamphlet; in Chambers, 189)

Chettle, Greene's publisher, apologizes to Shakespeare:

I am as sory as if the originall fault [the writing of the pamphlet] had beene my fault, because myselfe haue seene his [Shakespeare's] demeanor no lesse ciuill than he excellent in the qualitie he professes: Besides diuers of worship haue reported his vprightnes of dealing which argues his honesty and his facetious grace in writting, that aproues his Art.

Francis Meres, *Palladis Tamia: Wit's Treasury* (1598; book; in Chambers, 194)

In this collection of pithy sayings about art and philosophy, Meres compares the work of English writers (beginning with the time of Chaucer) to classic Greek, Latin, and Italian poets. He says of Shakespeare:

> As the soule of Euphorbus was thought to lie in Pythagoras: so the sweete wittie soule of Ovid lives in mellifluous and hony-tongued Shakespeare, witnes his Venus and Adonis, his Lucrece, his sugred Sonnets among his private friends, etc.
>
> As Plautus and Seneca are accounted the best for Comedy and Tragedy among the latines: so Shakespeare among the English is the most excellent, in both kinds for the stage: for Comedy, witness his *Gentlemen of Verona*, his *Errors*, his *Love's Labours Lost*, his *Love's Labours Wonne*, his *Midsummers Night Dream* and his *Merchant of Venice*; for Tragedy his *Richard the 2*, *Richard the 3*, *Henry the 4*, *King John*, *Titus Andronicus* and his *Romeo and Juliet*. As Epius Stolo said, that the Muses would speak with Plautus tongue, if they would speak Latin: so I say that the Muses would speak with Shakespeare's fine filed phrase, if they would speak English.

Parnassas 1, 2, 3 (1598, 1599, 1601; plays; in Chambers, 201)

These anonymous plays, written by students for performances at Cambridge at Christmastime 1598, 1599, and 1601, contain the following allusions to Shakespeare:

> Let this duncified world esteeme of Spencer and Chaucer, I'le worshippe sweet Mr. Shakespeare, and to honor him will lay his Venus and Adonis under my pillowe. (*2 Parnassas* [performed 1599, published 1609])

> Few of the university men pen plaies well, they smell too much of that writer Ovid and that writer Metamorphosis, and talk too much of

Proserpina and Iuppiter. Why here's our fellow Shakespeare puts them all down. (*3 Parnassas* [performed 1601, published 1609])

The above lines in *3 Parnassas* are spoken by a character named Kempe, an allusion to the Will Kempe of Shakespeare's company. Burbage is also a character in this play in which Shakespeare's *Richard III* is directly quoted.

John Davies, *Microcosmos* (1603; poem; in Chambers, 214)

In *Microcosmos*, Davies refers to W. S. as follows:

> And though the stage doth stain pure gentle blood,
> Yet generous ye are in mind and mood.

John Davies, *Scourge of Folly* (1610; book)

> To our English Terence, Mr. Will Shakespeare:
> Some say (good Will) which I, in sport do sing,
> Had'st thou not plaid some Kingly parts in sport,
> Thou had'st been a companion for a King;
> And been a King among the meaner sort.
> Some others raile, but raile as they think fit
> Thou hast no railing but a reigning wit.
> And honesty thou sow'st, which they do reape;
> So, to increase their Stocke which they do keepe.

Ben Jonson, poetic tribute in *First Folio of Shakespeare's Plays* (1623; in Halliday, *A Shakespeare Companion*, 142)

In this poem, Jonson describes the Droeshout portrait of Shakespeare, used as the frontispiece to the first printing of Shakespeare's collected plays.

> This Figure, that thou here seest put,
> It was for gentle Shakespeare cut:
> Wherein the Grauer had a strife
> With Nature, to out-doo the life:
> O, could he but haue drawne his wit
> As well in brass, as he hath hit

His face, the Print would then surpasse
All that was euer writ in brasse.
But since he cannot, Reader, looke
Not on his Picture, but his Booke.

Ben Jonson, second poetic tribute, also in *First Folio of Shakespeare's Plays* (1623; in Halliday, *A Shakespeare Companion*, 259)

To the memory of my beloved, the author Mr. William
    Shakespeare and what he has left us.
To draw no envy (Shakespeare) on thy name
Am I thus ample to thy Book, and Fame:
While I confess thy writings to be such,
As neither Man, nor Muse, can praise too much.
    Soul of the Age!
The applause! delight! the wonder of our Stage! ...
Triumph, my Britain, thou hast one to show,
To whom all Scenes of Europe homage owe.
He was not of an age, but for all time!
And all the Muses still were in their prime,
When like Apollo he came forth to warm
Our ears, or like a Mercury to charm.

Michael Drayton, *Elegy* (1627; in Halliday, *A Shakespeare Companion*, 142)

The following praise of Shakespeare is found in the middle of the poem *Elegy*, subtitled "To my most dearely-loved friend HENERY REYNOLDS Esquire, of *Poets & Poesie*," which was printed with Drayton's *The Battaile of Agincourt* in 1627:

And let it be said of thee,
Shakespeare, thou hadst as smooth a comicke vaine
Fitting the socke, and in thy naturall braine,
As strong conception, and as Cleere a rage,
As anyone that trafiqu'd with the stage.

Thomas Heywood, *The Hierarchie of the Blessed Angels* (1635; poem; in Halliday, *A Shakespeare Companion*, 226)

Nearly twenty years after Shakespeare's death, fellow playwright Heywood comments on the poet's talent and lack of pretension:

> Mellifluous Shakespeare, whose enchanting quill
> Commanded mirth or passion, was but Will.

Appendix C

Most Important Elizabethan/ Jacobean Dramatists and Actors

Dramatists

Wilson, Robert	c. 1550–c. 1605
Lyly, John	c. 1554–c. 1606
Lodge, Thomas	c. 1557–c. 1625
Peele, George	c. 1557–c. 1596
Greene, Robert	1558–1592
Kyd, Thomas	1558–1594
Barnes, Barnabe	c. 1559–1609
Chapman, George	c. 1560–1634
Chettle, Henry	c. 1560–1607
Munday, Anthony	c. 1560–1633
Daniel, Samuel	c. 1563–1619
Drayton, Michael	1563–1631
Marlowe, Christopher	1564–1593
Shakespeare, William	1564–1616
Nashe, Thomas	1567–c. 1601
Hathway, Richard	c. 1570–c. 1610

Middleton, Thomas	c. 1570–1627
Rowley, Samuel	c. 1570–c. 1630
Dekker, Thomas	c. 1572–c. 1632
Jonson, Benjamin	1572–1637
Heywood, Thomas	1573–1641
Day, John	c. 1574–c. 1640
Haughton, William	c. 1575–1605
Marston, John	c. 1575–1634
Tourneur, Cyril	c. 1575–1626
Fletcher, John	1579–1625
Daborne, Robert	c. 1580–1628
Rowley, William	c. 1580–c. 1635
Webster, John	c. 1580–c. 1630
Massinger, Philip	1583–1640
Beaumont, Francis	1584–1616
Ford, John	1586–c. 1639

Source: F. E. Halliday, *A Shakespeare Companion*, 1564–1964 (Harmondsworth, Middlesex, England: Penguin Books, 1964), 141.

Actors in Shakespeare's company (as listed in the First Folio, 1623)

William Shakespeare	Samuel Gilburne
Richard Burbage	Robert Armin
John Heminges	William Ostler
Augustine Phillips	Nathan Field
Will Kempe	John Underwood
Thomas Pope	Nicholas Tooley
George Bryan	William Ecclestone
Henry Condell	Robert Benfield
William Sly	Richard Gough
Richard Cowly	Richard Robinson
John Lowine	Lawrence Fletcher
Samuel Cross	John Duke
Alexander Cooke	Christopher Beeston
James Sands	

Appendix D

Revisiting Baldwin: Roles the Friends Played

╫══ ══╫

In his book *The Organization and Personnel of the Shakespearean Company*, T. W. Baldwin attempts by meticulous inductive reasoning to determine what roles each member of Shakespeare's companies most logically might have played. He starts with records of roles attributed to given members of the company in plays by Ben Jonson (where cast lists have been preserved). Baldwin also examines accidental references to actor names in Shakespearean plays, where the name of the actor Kempe, for instance, is substituted for the character name Peter in the second quarto printing of *Romeo and Juliet*. The name Kempe is also substituted for the character name Dogberry at the head of one speech in the quarto version of *Much Ado About Nothing*, confirming William Kempe's role as the leading clown actor in the company. From such indications Baldwin analyzes the "line of business" (that is, what sort of character) each actor typically played. He then traces this type of role through the Shakespeare canon, and makes the logical assumption that the actor who originally played a certain type of role would continue to play that type or "line" throughout his career. His reasoning is persuasive. Though no one can say each instance of his casting is correct, his lists give us insight into the personalities of the actors and the organization of the company, so his theories in broad outline are convincing. His conclusions on casting for Shakespeare and his closest friends Richard Burbage, John Heminges, and Henry Condell are as follows:

Roles played by **Richard Burbage** in Shakespeare's plays:

Hamlet, Prince Hal, Richard III, Talbot, Henry V, Richard II, John, Brutus, Lucentio, Bassanio, Claudio (*Much Ado About Nothing*), Orlando, Berowne, Orsino, Lear, Antony, Ford, Othello, Angelo, Timon, Demetrius, Fenton, Lucius, Romeo, Wolsey, Prospero, Macbeth, Bertram, Pericles, Coriolanus, Postumos, Leontes

Baldwin describes Burbage's line of business as the hero or the leading man.

Roles played by **John Heminges**:

Boyet, Lafeu, Aegeon, Duke of Milan, Capulet, Polonius, Leonato, Brabatio, Marcus, Egeus, York, Glendower, Duke Senior, Kent, Exeter, Gloucester, Hastings, Hubert, Chief Justice, Corambis

Baldwin describes Heminges' "line," as the older character man.

Roles played by **Henry Condell**:

Paris, Don Pedro, Antony, Oliver, Antonio, Constable, Edgar, Malcolm, Caesar, Simonides, Northumberland, Salisbury, Duke (*Measure for Measure*), Gratiano, King (*All's Well That Ends Well*), Tranio

Condell probably took over the following roles formerly played by George Bryan:

The King, Friar Laurence, Young Henry VI, Bassianus (*Titus Andronicus*), Richmond, Eglamour, Lysander, Cominius, Belarius, Buckingham, Canterbury, Page, Horatio

Condell is thought to have been an apprentice of Heminges. Baldwin describes his line as the "dignified young man."

Roles played by **William Shakespeare**:

Ghost, Adam, Duncan, Lepidus, Friar Peter, Charles VI, Duke (*All's Well That Ends Well, Othello, Love's Labours Won, The Comedy of Errors, Romeo and Juliet, The Merchant of Venice*), Antonio, Vincentio, Friar Francis, Sea Captain, Cinna, Cicero, Nathaniel

Baldwin notes that these small roles of limited requirements place Shakespeare in a position to oversee rehearsals and performances.

Notes

Introduction

1. Caroline Spurgeon, *Shakespeare's Imagery and What It Tells Us* (Cambridge: Cambridge University Press, 1966), 207, 208.

William Shakespeare

1. E. K. Chambers, *William Shakespeare, A Study of Facts and Problems*, vol. 2 (Oxford: Clarendon Press, 1930), 188.

2. Ibid., 263.

Shakespeare's Stratford Friends

1. Robert Payne, *By Me, William Shakespeare* (New York: Everest House, 1980), 6.

2. Marchette Chute, *Shakespeare of London* (New York: E. P. Dutton, 1949), 333.

Richard Quiney

3. Samuel Schoenbaum, *William Shakespeare, A Compact Documentary Life* (New York: Oxford University Press, 1987), 237.

4. Ibid., 239.

5. Chambers, 103.

6. Schoenbaum, *William Shakespeare*, 239, 240.

7. Alan Palmer and Veronica Palmer, *Who's Who in Shakespeare's England* (New York: St. Martin's Press, 1999), 198.

Richard Field

8. C. C. Stopes, *Shakespeare's Warwickshire Contemporaries* (Stratford-upon-Avon: Shakespeare Head Press, 1907), 10.

9. Ian Wilson, *Shakespeare, The Evidence* (New York: St. Martin's Press, 1993), 219.

10. Stopes, *Shakespeare's Warwickshire*, 13.

11. A. L. Rowse, *William Shakespeare, A Biography* (New York: Harper & Row, 1963), 62.

12. Mark Bland, "The London Book Trade I, 1600," in *A Companion to Shakespeare*, ed. David Scott Kastan (Oxford: Blackwell Publishers, 1999), 450.

13. Laurie E. Maguire, "The Craft of Printing (1600)," in Kastan, 434.

The Combe Family

14. Rowse, *William Shakespeare*, 450.

15. Schoenbaum, *William Shakespeare*, 283.

16. Ibid., 284.

17. Ibid., 285.

18. Ibid., 243.

19. Ian Wilson, 380, 381.

The Nash Family

20. Rowse, *William Shakespeare*, 465.

Thomas Greene

21. Chambers, 142, 143.

John Hall

22. Chute, *Shakespeare of London*, 295.

23. Anthony Burgess, *Shakespeare* (Harmondsworth, Middlesex: Penguin Books, 1972), 236.

24. Chambers, 11.

Thomas Russell

25. Ibid., 231.

Alexander Aspinall

26. Rowse, *William Shakespeare*, 23.
27. Ibid., 24.
28. Schoenbaum, *William Shakespeare*, 67.

John Robinson

29. Ian Wilson, 396.

Francis Collins

30. Chambers, 170.

Queen Elizabeth I

1. Peter Quennell, *Shakespeare, A Biography* (Cleveland: The World Publishing Company, 1963), 74, 75.
2. Chambers, 326.
3. Ibid., 209.

Henry Wriothesley, the Earl of Southampton

4. Ian Wilson, 135.
5. Park Honan, *Shakespeare, A Life* (New York: Oxford University Press, 1998), 179.
6. Ian Wilson, 274.
7. William Shakespeare, *Sonnet 107*, in *The Complete Works of William Shakespeare*. The Cambridge text established by John Dover Wilson for Cambridge University Press (London: Octopus Books Limited, 1980), 1140.
8. Ian Wilson, 305.

Emilia Bassano Lanier

9. A. L. Rowse, *The Poems of Shakespeare's Dark Lady* (New York: Clarkson N. Potter, Inc., 1979), 29.
10. Ibid., 48.
11. Ibid., 20.
12. Ibid., 137.

The Earls and the Countess of Pembroke

13. Sir Philip Sidney, *The Old Arcadia* (Oxford: Oxford University Press, 1985), 3.
14. Palmer, 187.
15. Ian Wilson, 400.

Lady Warwick

16. Violet Wilson, *Society Women of Shakespeare's Time* (London: The Bodley Head Limited, 1924), 140.
17. Ibid., 141.

Maria Mountjoy

18. Schoenbaum, *William Shakespeare*, 262.

William Johnson

19. F. E. Halliday, *A Shakespeare Companion 1564–1964* (Harmondsworth, Middlesex, England: Penguin Books, 1964), 117.
20. Palmer, 54.
21. Chambers, 252.

Michael Drayton

22. Oliver Elton, *Michael Drayton: An Introduction to Michael Drayton* (New York: B. Franklin, 1970), 49.
23. Palmer, 163.

Philip Henslowe

1. Halliday, *A Shakespeare Companion*, 221.
2. Ibid.
3. Ibid.

Edward Alleyn

4. Ian Wilson, 8.
5. Chute, *Shakespeare of London*, 127.

Christopher Marlowe

6. Algernon Charles Swinburne, "Marlowe, Christopher," in *The Encyclopedia Britannica*, 11th ed., vol. 17 (Cambridge: Cambridge University Press, 1911), 741.

7. Michael Wood, *Shakespeare* (New York: Basic Books, 2003), 154.

8. Christopher Marlowe, "The Passionate Shepherd to His Love," in *The Oxford Book of English Verse*, ed. Sir Arthur Quiller-Couch (Oxford: Clarendon Press, 1957), 179.

9. Christopher Marlowe, *Dr. Faustus*, scene 13, line 90, in *The Complete Plays*, ed. Frank Romany and Robert Lindsey (London: Penguin Books, 2003), lines 90–104, 390.

10. Ibid., scene 14, lines 62–73, 393.

11. William Shakespeare, *As You Like It*, act 3, scene 5, lines 81–82, in *The Complete Works of William Shakespeare*, ed. John Dover Wilson, 258.

12. Marlowe, *Tamburlaine the Great, Part 1*, act 2, scene 3, lines 14–24, in *The Complete Plays*, ed. Romany and Lindsey, 95.

Ben Jonson

13. Ben Jonson, "To Celia," in *Ben Jonson and the Cavalier Poets*, ed. Hugh Maclean (New York: Norton, 1974), 28.

14. Marchette Chute, *Ben Jonson of Westminster* (New York: E. P. Dutton, 1949), 11.

15. Halliday, *A Shakespeare Companion*, 258.

16. Chute, *Ben Jonson of Westminster*, 44.

17. Ibid., 45.

18. Ben Jonson, "On My First Son," in *Ben Jonson and the Cavalier Poets*, ed. Maclean, 8.

19. Ibid., "Epitaph on S. P.," 13.

20. Chambers, 245.

21. Halliday, *A Shakespeare Companion*, 354.

22. Chambers, 210.

23. Ibid., 208.

Thomas Dekker

24. Halliday, *A Shakespeare Companion*, 200.

25. Shakespeare, *Hamlet*, act 2, scene 2, lines 348–370, in *The Complete Works of William Shakespeare*, ed. John Dover Wilson, 897.

Beaumont and Fletcher

26. Halliday, *A Shakespeare Companion*, 57.

Francis Beaumont

27. Chambers, 224.

Shareholders and Housekeepers

28. Halliday, *A Shakespeare Companion*, 185.

Thomas Pope

29. Ibid., 381.

William Sly

30. Halliday, *A Shakespeare Companion*, 458.
31. Ibid., 32.

Cuthbert Burbage

32. Schoenbaum, *William Shakespeare*, 208.
33. Halliday, *A Shakespeare Companion*, 449.
34. Ibid., 498.

Will Kempe

35. Ibid., 263.
36. Palmer and Palmer, 139.

Augustine Phillips

37. Halliday, *A Shakespeare Companion*, 366.
38. Chambers, 325. The date on this document is 1600. In England at this time, the year changed in March, not January.
39. Halliday, *A Shakespeare Companion*, 367.
40. Ibid.

Richard Burbage

41. Ibid., 77.
42. William Shakespeare, *Henry V*, act 4, scene 8, line 125.
43. Charles Connell, *They Gave Us Shakespeare* (Stocksfield: Oriel Press, 1982), 37.
44. Chute, *Shakespeare of London*, 217.
45. Halliday, *A Shakespeare Companion*, 77.
46. Rowse, *William Shakespeare*, 455.
47. Chute, *Shakespeare of London*, 324.
48. Rowse, *William Shakespeare*, 455–456.
49. Halliday, *A Shakespeare Companion*, 77.

John Heminges

    50. Payne, 380, 381.

The First Folio

    1. Chambers, 228.
    2. Payne, 422.
    3. Chambers, 228–230.

Selected Bibliography

Akrigg, G.P.V. *Shakespeare and the Earl of Southampton*. Cambridge: Harvard University Press, 1968.

Appleton, William W. *Beaumont and Fletcher, A Critical Study*. London: Allen and Unwin, 1956.

Asimov, Isaac. *Asimov's Guide to Shakespeare*. New York: Avenel Books, 1978.

Aubrey, John. *Brief Lives*. Edited by Oliver Lawson Dick. London: Seekes and Warburg, 1949.

Baldwin, T. W. *The Organization and Personnel of the Shakespearean Company*. Princeton: Princeton University Press, 1927.

Barroll, J. Leeds, et al. *The Revels History of Drama in English*. Vol. 3, *1576–1613*. London: Methuen, 1975.

Bartlett, John. *Familiar Quotations*. Boston: Little, Brown and Company, 1980.

Bloom, Harold. *Shakespeare: The Invention of the Human*. New York: Riverhead Books, 1998.

Boyce, Charles. *Shakespeare A to Z*. New York: Roundtable Press, 1990.

Brown, Ivor. *How Shakespeare Spent the Day*. New York: Hill and Wang, 1963.

Burgess, Anthony. *Shakespeare*. Harmondsworth, Middlesex: Penguin Books, 1972.

Chambers, E. K. *William Shakespeare, A Study of Facts and Problems*. 2 vols. Oxford: Clarendon Press, 1930.

Chute, Marchette. *Ben Jonson of Westminster*. New York: E. P. Dutton, 1960.
———. *Shakespeare of London*. New York: E. P. Dutton, 1949.
Connell, Charles. *They Gave Us Shakespeare*. Stocksfield: Oriel Press, 1982.
Cooper, Duff. *Sergeant Shakespeare*. New York: Viking Press, 1950.
Dunn, Esther Cloudman, ed. *Eight Famous Elizabethan Plays*. New York: The Modern Library, 1950.
Elton, Oliver. *Michael Drayton: An Introduction to Michael Drayton*. New York: B. Franklin, 1970.
Folger Shakespeare Library. Exhibition on the Elizabethan Book Trade. Washington, D.C.: Exhibition Gallery, Winter, 2002.
Fripp, Edgar. *Master Richard Quyny*. London: Oxford University Press, 1924.
———. *Shakespeare Man and Artist*. 2 vols. London: Oxford University Press, 1938.
Giroux, Robert. *The Book Known as Q*. New York: Vintage Books, 1982.
Godley, Robert J. *Southwark, A History of Bankside, Bermondsey and "The Borough."* London: Robert J. Godley in collaboration with the Southwark Heritage Association, 1996.
Gollob, Herman. *Me and Shakespeare*. New York: Doubleday, 2002.
Greenblatt, Stephen. *Will in the World*. New York: W.W. Norton, 2004.
Halliday, F. E. *Shakespeare*. 1956. Reprint, New York: Thames and Hudson, 1998.
———. *A Shakespeare Companion 1564–1964*. Harmondsworth, Middlesex, England: Penguin Books, 1964.
Harbage, Alfred. *Sir William Davanant*. Philadelphia: University of Pennsylvania Press, 1935.
Honan, Park. *Shakespeare, A Life*. New York: Oxford University Press, 1998.
Jameson, Thomas. *The Hidden Shakespeare*. New York: Funk and Wagnalls, 1967.
Kastan, David Scott, ed. *A Companion to Shakespeare*. Oxford: Blackwell Publishers, 1999.
Leech, Clifford. *The John Fletcher Plays*. Cambridge: Harvard University Press, 1962.
Lomonico, Michael. *The Shakespeare Book of Lists*. Franklin Lakes, N.J.: The Career Press, Inc., 2001.
Macardle, Dorothy. *Shakespeare, Man and Boy*. London: Faber and Faber, 1961.
Maclean, Hugh. *Ben Jonson and the Cavalier Poets*. New York: Norton, 1974.
Marlowe, Christopher. *The Complete Plays*. Edited by Frank Romany and Robert Lindsey. London: Penguin Books, 2003.
Muir, K., and S. Schoenbaum. "The Life of Shakespeare." In *A New Companion to Shakespeare Studies*. Cambridge: Cambridge University Press, 1971.
Nethercot, Arthur H. *Sir William Davanant, Poet Laureate and Playwright-Manager*. Chicago: University of Chicago Press, 1938.
Newdigate, Bernard H. *Michael Drayton and His Circle*. Oxford: Shakespeare Head Press, B. Blackwell, Publisher, 1941.

Palmer, Alan, and Veronica Palmer. *Who's Who in Shakespeare's England.* New York: St. Martin's Press, 1999.

Parks, Edd Winfield, and Richmond Croom Beatty. *The English Drama, An Anthology 900–1642.* New York: W.W. Norton, 1935.

Payne, Robert. *By Me, William Shakespeare.* New York: Everest House, 1980.

Phelps, William Lyon. *Christopher Marlowe. Masterpieces of the English Drama.* New York: American Book Company, 1912.

Quennell, Peter. *Shakespeare, A Biography.* Cleveland: The World Publishing Company, 1963.

Quiller-Couch, Sir Arthur, ed. *The Oxford Book of English Verse 1250–1918.* Oxford: Clarendon Press, 1957.

Rowse, A. L. *The Poems of Shakespeare's Dark Lady.* New York: Clarkson N. Potter, Inc., 1979.

———. *Shakespeare's Sonnets: The Problem Solved.* New York: Harper & Row, 1964, 1973.

———. *Shakespeare's Southampton, patron of Virginia.* New York: Harper & Row, 1965.

———. *William Shakespeare, A Biography.* New York: Harper & Row, 1963.

Schoenbaum, Samuel. *Shakespeare's Lives.* London: Oxford University Press, 1991.

———. *William Shakespeare, A Compact Documentary Life.* New York: Oxford University Press, 1987.

Shakespeare, William. *The Complete Works of William Shakespeare.* The Cambridge text established by John Dover Wilson for the Cambridge University Press. London: Octopus Books Limited, 1980.

Sidney, Sir Philip. *The Old Arcadia.* Oxford: Oxford University Press, 1985.

Sitwell, Edith. *English Women.* London: Prion, 1997.

Sobel, Bernard. *The Theatre Handbook.* New York: Crown Publishers, 1940.

Spurgeon, Caroline. *Shakespeare's Imagery, and What It Tells Us.* Cambridge: Cambridge University Press, 1966.

Squier, Charles L. *John Fletcher.* Boston: Twayne Publishers, 1986.

Sternfeld, F. W. *Music in Shakespeare's Tragedy.* London: Routledge and Paul, 1963.

Stevenson, Burton. *The Home Book of Quotations.* New York: Dodd, Mead & Company, 1952.

Stopes, C. C. *The Life of Henry, the Third Earl of Southampton.* 2nd ed. 1922. Reprint, New York: AMS Press, 1969.

———. *Shakespeare's Warwickshire Contemporaries.* Stratford-upon-Avon: Shakespeare Head Press, 1907.

Wilson, Ian. *Shakespeare, The Evidence.* New York: St. Martin's Press, 1993.

Wilson, Violet. *Society Women of Shakespeare's Time.* London: The Bodley Head Limited, 1924.

Wood, Michael. *Shakespeare.* New York: Basic Books, 2003.

Index

Act of Vagabondage, 56
Acting Companies:
—Admiral's Men, 67, 84, 87, 91, 109–10; Jonson as playwright, 95
—Chamberlain's Men, 4, 5, 6, 27, 50, 51, 53, 67, 68, 109–11; Beaumont and Fletcher as playwrights, 104; Essex uprising performance, 120; Jonson as playwright, 95; Theatre, razing, 124–25; Will Kempe, member, 116
—King's Men, 5, 7, 53, 62, 70, 109–11; Blackfriars performances, 125; Burbage as leading actor, 126; Heminges as member, 129; Jonson as playwright, 95, 96
—Leicester's Men, 3, 117
—Lord Derby's Men, 67, 109
—Lord Strange's Men, 50, 67, 68, 85, 87, 109; Augustine Phillips, member, 121; John Heminges, member, 129; Will Kempe, member, 117
—Pembroke's Men, 66, 68, 69
—Queen's Men, 3, 55, 67, 129; Will Kempe, member,117
—Warwick's Men, 72
—Worcester's Men, 87, 118
Admiral's Men. *See* Acting Companies
Allen, Giles, 114, 124
Alleyn, Constance Donne, 86, 88
Alleyn, Edward, 4, 68, 78, 83, 84, 85–89; death, 89, 123; reputation based on Marlowe, 91; rivalry with Burbage, 109–11; tour with Heminge, 129
Alleyn, Joan Henslowe, 86, 88
Alleyn, John, 124
Armin, Robert, 119
Aspinall, Alexander, 8, 40–41, 143, 145

Aspinall, Ann Shaw, 41, 42, 132
Aubrey, John, 76, 105

Bassano family, 63
Beaumont, Francis, 76, 100, 104–6
Beeston, Christopher, 76, 122
Beeston, William, 76
Belott, Stephen, 7, 74
Bishop, George, 22
Blackfriars Gatehouse. *See* London:
    Blackfriars Gatehouse
Blackfriars Theatre. *See* London:
    Blackfriars Theatre
Brayne, John, 124
Browne, Robert, 112–13
Bryan, George, 4, 67, 87, 109, 125
Burbage, Cuthbert, 110–11, 113–16,
    124, 125, 126
Burbage, James, 3, 48, 68, 74,
    109–11, 114, 115, 123, 124, 125
Burbage, Richard, 3, 4, 7, 45, 46,
    62, 122–28, 129; actor, 50, 67,
    71, 93, 127; Chamberlain's
    Men, founding, 125; death,
    127, 128; family, 126; King's
    Men, 126; painter, 123;
    Phillips' bequest, 122; roles
    played, 124; Shakespeare's
    bequest, 45, 144; shareholder,
    109–11, 115, 144; wife, 126
Burbage, Winifred, 126, 133–35
Burghley, Lord. *See* Cecil, William

Carey, Henry, Lord Hunsdon
    (Lord Chamberlain), 4, 63,
    109–11; Chamberlain's Men,
    founding, 125
Cecil, William, Lord Burghley, 57,
    59
Chamberlain, Lord. *See* Carey,
    Henry
Chamberlain's Men. *See* Acting
    Companies
Chapman, George, 94, 107

Clifford, Anne, 71, 72
Clopton, Sir Hugh, 39
Collaboration in playwriting, 79
Collins, Francis, 8, 33, 42, 43–45
Combe, John, 27–30, 33, 44, 45, 145
Combe, Thomas, 6, 27–30
Combe, William, 6, 27–30, 33
Condell, Elizabeth, 133–35
Condell, Henry, 6, 39, 45, 71, 129,
    131; First Folio, 137–42;
    monument, 130; Phillips'
    bequest, 122; Shakespeare's
    bequest, 45, 144; shareholder,
    111, 144
Cooke, James, 35, 37
Coryat, Thomas, 76
Cowley, Richard, 109, 116, 125

Dark Lady, 63, 65, 70, 88. *See also*
    Lanier, Emilia Bassano
Davenant, Jane, 80, 81
Davenant, John, 80
Davenant, Robert, 80, 81, 145
Davenant, William, 46, 80–81
Dekker, Thomas, 33, 68, 100,
    101–4; plays, 101–2; War of the
    Theatres, 96, 102–3
Derby's Men. *See* Acting Companies
Devereux, Robert, Earl of Essex, 6,
    51, 58, 61; execution, 121;
    Richard II, request to play, 120
Digges, Anne. *See* Russell, Anne
    Digges
Digges, Dudley, 39, 134
Digges, Leonard, 39, 134
Digges, Thomas, 39
Donne, Constance, 86, 88
Donne, John, 86, 88
Drayton, Michael, 8, 68, 76,
    77–80, 84; Beaumont, friend
    to, 105
Dudley, Robert, Earl of Leicester,
    9, 71, 72
Dulwich College, 89

Elizabeth I, 5, 6, 9, 15, 49, 50–53, 61, 68; Alleyn's retirement, displeasure with, 87; command performances, 110; Essex, quarrel with, 120; Wilton House, visit to, 70
Essex, Earl of. *See* Devereux, Robert

Field, Jacqueline Vautrollier, 22, 73, 132, 133, 135
Field, Jasper, 23
Field, Richard, 2, 9, 11, 13, 22–27, 73, 74, 125
First Folio, 88, 130, 137–42
Fitton, Mary, 70
Fletcher, John, 76, 100, 104–5, 107–8; collaborations with Shakespeare, 107, 108
Fletcher, Lawrence, 54, 110, 122
Florio, John (Giovanni), 62
Forman, Simon, 64, 74
Friday Street Club, 76

Globe Theatre. *See* London: Globe Theatre
Gorboduc, 58
Gray's Inn. *See* London: Inns of Court
Green, Peter, 114
Greene, Robert, 3, 106, 144
Greene, Thomas, 8, 16; children, 33, 46; Welcombe enclosure 28, 29, 32–34
Greville, Sir Edward, 15, 16
Guild Hall, 19
Gunpowder Plot, 19

Hall, Elizabeth, 8, 17, 31, 43, 46
Hall, John, 8, 16, 34–38, 43; casebook, 36; daughter, 36, 38; education, 35; epitaph, 38; executor to Shakespeare's will, 36, 45; home, 35; marriage, 34, 37; Michael Drayton as patient, 78; other patients, 35; religion, 36; treatments, 35, 36; will, 31, 38
Hall's Croft, 35
Harington, Sir John, 51, 54
Harrison, John, 25, 27
Hathaway, Anne, 2, 8, 43; second-best bed, 45
Heminges, John, 4, 6, 39, 45, 46, 129–30; actor, 87; Chamberlain's Men, founding, 125; Condell as apprentice, 131; dedication of First Folio, 71, 137–42; family, 129; grocer, 130; Phillips' bequest, 122; roles played, 129; Shakespeare's bequest, 45, 144; shareholder, 109–11, 115, 144; trustee of Blackfriars Gatehouse, 77
Heminges, Rebecca, 129, 133, 134, 135
Heminges, Thomasine, 129
Heminges, William, 46, 129
Henry VIII, 18, 19, 26
Henslowe, Philip, 4, 48, 68, 78, 83–85, 86, 109–11; Dekker, support of, 101; Jonson, loan to, 95; Sly, sale of jewel, 112
Herbert, Henry, 2nd Earl of Pembroke, 4, 66, 69
Herbert, Philip, 4th Earl of Pembroke, 72, 138
Herbert, William, 3rd Earl of Pembroke, 70, 128, 138
Heywood, Thomas, 68, 113
Hunsdon, Baron. *See* Carey, Henry

Inner Temple. *See* London: Inns of Court
Inns of Court. *See* London: Inns of Court

James I, 6, 7, 18, 49, 50, 51, 53–55, 62, 131; invited to Wilton, 70
Johnson, William, 6, 75–77

Jonson, Ben, 8, 10, 68, 93–99, 104, 107; apprentices, 95; children, 94, 95; epitaph, 30; Friday Street Club, member, 76; looks, 96; masques, 97; "merry meeting" anecdote, 78, 98; Pembroke as patron, 71; personality, 144; play writing theory, 96, 97; plays, 95, 97; schooling, 94; War of the Theatres, 33, 96, 102–3; wife, 94; wit-combats with Shakespeare, 96; writings on Shakespeare, 53, 98, 99

Kempe, Will, 4, 87, 108–12, 115, 116–19, 144; Chamberlain's Men, founding, 125; *Kempe's Nine Daies Wonder*, 116
King's Men. *See* Acting Companies
Knell, William, 67, 129
Kyd, Thomas, 69, 90, 144

Lanier, Emilia Bassano, 63–66
Leicester, Earl of. *See* Dudley, Robert
Leicester's Men. *See* Acting Companies
London (and environs), 47–48, 49
—Aldermanbury, 74, 129
—Bankside, 84, 126
—Bearbaiting and cockfighting, 5, 73
—Bishopsgates Street, 4
—Blackfriars, 7, 22
—Blackfriars Gatehouse, 7, 22, 42, 77, 130, 145
—Blackfriars Theatre, 7, 74, 110–11, 116, 125, 140
—books and booksellers, 24, 26
—the Clink, 4, 73
—Cross Keys Inn, 110
—Curtain Theatre, 4, 114
—Finsbury Fields, 4, 27, 114

—Fortune Theatre, 78, 84, 88
—Globe Theatre, 5, 73, 78, 110, 113, 115, 118, 121, 125, 129, 133
—Halliwell (Holywell), 114, 115, 123, 126
—Hope Theatre, 84
—Inns of Court, 57–58; Gray's Inn, 106, 110; Inner Temple, 105
—London Bridge, 48
—Marshalsea Prison, 15
—Monkwell (Mugwell) Street, 73
—Newington Butts Theatre, 84, 109, 125
—the plague, 4, 56
—population, 47
—river, 47
—Rose Theatre, 48, 68, 73, 78, 84, 109
—Shoreditch Road, 4, 27, 123
—Silver Street, 6, 24, 73, 74
—Southwark, 4, 84
—St. Mary Aldermanbury, 74, 130
—St. Olave's, 6, 24, 73
—St. Paul's, 26, 48, 78
—Swan Theatre, 68, 110
—The Theatre, 4, 48, 67, 109, 114, 123, 125
—the Tower, 48
Lord Derby's Men. *See* Acting Companies
Lord Strange's Men. *See* Acting Companies

Manners, Francis, 6th Earl of Rutland, 7, 123
Manningham, John, 127
Marlowe, Christopher, 4, 58, 60, 68, 69, 83, 144; papers at Dulwich, 89–93; writing for Edward Alleyn, 87
Marston, John, 33, 102–3
Meres, Francis, 79
Mermaid Tavern, 6, 19, 74, 76

Mountjoy, Christopher, 6, 7, 24, 73, 74, 75

Mountjoy, Maria, 6, 7, 24, 64, 73–75

Mountjoy, Mary, 74

Nash, Anthony, 8, 30–31, 33, 45

Nash, Dorothy, 31

Nash, John, 8, 30–31, 32, 45

Nash, Thomas, 8, 30–31

New Place, 5, 6, 18; description, 33; Halls' residence, 36; Thomas Greene in, 32, 33

Ostler, William, 129

Pembroke, Countess of. *See* Sidney, Mary

Pembroke, Earl of. *See* Herbert, Henry

Pembroke family, 66–71

Pembroke's Men. *See* Acting Companies

Phillips, Augustine, 4, 50, 67, 87, 113, 119–22; Chamberlain's Men, founding, 125; Condell, bequest to, 131; performance, 120–21; shareholder, 115, 118; testimony about *Richard II*, 120; will, 122

Pope, Thomas, 4, 50, 67, 87, 109, 111–12; Chamberlain's Men, founding, 125; shareholder, 115, 118

Pyk, John, 86

Queen's Men. *See* Acting Companies

Quiney, Elizabeth (Bess), 8, 16, 132, 135

Quiney, George, 16

Quiney, Richard, 2, 6, 9, 13–17, 18, 27; children, 14, 16; death, 16; education, 13; father, 13; imprisonment, 15; letter to Shakespeare, 14; public service, 13, 15; wife, 13; work, 13

Quiney, Thomas, 8, 16, 44

Religion, 18–19, 31, 32; Puritanism, 117

Reynolds, William, 8, 31–32, 45

Robinson, John, 42–43, 45

Rose Theatre. *See* London: Rose Theatre

Russell, Anne, Lady Warwick, 71–73

Russell, Anne Digges, 39, 40, 132, 134, 135

Russell, Thomas, 8, 38–40, 44, 132, 134

Rutland, Earl of. *See* Manners, Francis

Sadler, Hamnet, 2, 3, 9, 11, 13, 17–20, 27; children, 17, 46; father, 17; financial difficulties, 18, 20, 30; religion, 18, 19; wife (*see* Sadler, Judith), 3, 17, 18; witness to Shakespeare's will, 20, 21, 42, 45

Sadler, Judith, 3, 19, 20, 132, 134, 135; missed Easter sacrament, 18

Sands, James, 122

Shakespeare, Edmund, 2, 7, 40, 108

Shakespeare, Hamnet, 3, 5, 17, 46

Shakespeare, John, 1, 2, 6, 22, 46; political life, 1, 55; profession, 10, 55; religion, 19

Shakespeare, Judith, 3, 8, 17, 43, 44

Shakespeare, Mary, 1

Shakespeare, Susanna, 3, 8, 17, 43; action for slander, 42; Blackfriars Gatehouse, 77; missed Easter sacrament, 18, 32; Shakespeare's legatee, 31, 44, 45; wife to John Hall, 38

Shakespeare, William: actor, 4, 6, 14, 126; Belott-Mountjoy lawsuit, 7, 75, 145; Chamberlain's Men, founding, 125; children, 3, 5, 8, 18, 145; coat of arms, 5, 145; Combe, John, epitaph, 29, 145; death, 8, 43; education, 2, 10–13; First Folio dedication, 138, 139; investments, 28, 29, 33, 72, 145; marriage, 2, 8, 12, 17, 18; not a company keeper, 76, 144; parents, 1, 6, 10, 12; Phillips' bequest, 122; portrayal of doctors, 37; Quiney loan request, 15; reading and books, 24, 40; religion, 19; residences, 5, 6, 7, 26, 32, 73; retirement, 7, 8, 18; Rutland *impresa*, 123, 128; shareholder, 4, 8, 68, 109–11, 115, 118, 144; siblings, 2, 7; source for characters in plays of others, 103–4; temperament, 144; travel, dislike of, 118, 119; Welcombe enclosure, 27, 33; will, 16, 43–44

Shakespeare, William, plays of:
—*All's Well That Ends Well*, 6, 137
—*Antony and Cleopatra*, 6, 7, 137
—*As You Like It*, 6, 60, 70, 92, 118, 129, 137
—*Comedy of Errors*, 4, 110, 137
—*Coriolanus*, 6, 137
—*Cymbeline*, 7, 105, 137, 144
—*Hamlet*, 6, 12, 16, 25, 51, 56, 103, 112, 117–18, 127, 129, 131
—*Henry IV, Parts 1 and 2*, 5, 50, 79
—*Henry V*, 6, 25, 49, 104
—*Henry VI* (three parts), 3, 4, 49, 55, 66, 67, 68, 85, 87, 137
—*Henry VIII*, 7, 52, 100, 107, 108, 137, 144
—*Julius Caesar*, 5, 7, 12, 104, 131, 137

—*King John*, 5, 49, 137
—*King Lear*, 6, 37, 131, 144
—*Love's Labours Lost*, 4, 12, 25, 40, 62–63
—*Macbeth*, 6, 37, 49, 54, 131, 137
—*Measure for Measure*, 6, 137
—*Midsummer Night's Dream, A*, 4, 51, 129
—*Merchant of Venice, The*, 5, 60
—*Merry Wives of Windsor, The*, 5, 12, 50, 92, 102
—*Much Ado About Nothing*, 6, 60, 117
—*Othello*, 6
—*Pericles*, 37, 100
—*Richard II*, 6, 49, 51, 118, 145; Essex uprising, 120
—*Richard III*, 4I, 49, 127
—*Romeo and Juliet*, 4, 117
—*Taming of the Shrew, The*, 4, 56, 11, 119, 137
—*Tempest, The*, 7, 137, 144
—*Timon of Athens*, 6, 137
—*Titus Andronicus*, 4, 7, 12, 66, 67, 68, 92
—*Troilus and Cressida*, 6, 7, 51
—*Twelfth Night*, 6, 60, 119, 127, 137
—*Two Gentlemen of Verona, The*, 4, 60, 119, 137
—*Two Noble Kinsmen, The*, 107
—*Winter's Tale, The*, 7, 119, 137, 144

Shakespeare, William, poems of: *Rape of Lucrece, The*, 4, 22, 25, 27, 56, 59, 144; *Sonnets*, 4, 59–60, 65, 66, 88, 93, 144; *Venus and Adonis*, 4, 22, 25, 27, 57, 59, 144
Shaw, Ann, 41
Shaw, Julius, 8, 32, 41–42, 45
Sidney, Mary, 69
Sidney, Sir Philip, 48, 69, 70
Slater, Martin, 79

Sly, William, 50, 67, 111, 112–13, 116
Southampton, Earl of. *See* Wriostheley, Henry
Spencer, Gabriel, 95
St. Paul's Cathedral. *See* London: St. Paul's
Stationer's Guild, 24, 25
Stationer's Register, 117, 138
Stratford, 1, 9; Corporation, 1, 42, 45; market, 10; population, 10; recreation, 10; trades, 10; trees, 9
Stratford Grammar School, 11; schoolmasters, 12
Street, Peter, 87
Sturley, Abraham, 14, 15

Tarleton, Richard, 67, 117
The Theatre. *See* London: The Theatre
Tooley, Nicholas, 116, 126, 131
Tyler, Richard, 2, 9, 13, 20–23, 27, 46

Vautrollier, Jacqueline. *See* Field, Jacqueline Vautrollier
Vautrollier, Thomas, 22
Vere, Elizabeth, 58
Vernon, Elizabeth, 58–59

Walker, Henry, 46
Walker, William, 45, 46
Warwick, Lady Anne. *See* Russell, Anne
Warwick's Men. *See* Acting Companies
Welcombe enclosure, 28, 33
Whatcott, Robert, 42, 45
Whateley, Anne, 2
Wheeler, Margaret, 44
Whyte, Rowland, 61
Willoughby, Ambrose, 58
Wilton House, 70, 121
Worcester's Men. *See* Acting Companies
Wriothesley, Henry, Earl of Southampton, 4, 6, 25, 51, 55–63, 64, 120

About the Author

KATE EMERY POGUE is Adjunct Professor in the Department of Drama at the University of Houston Downtown. She is a playwright, Shakespearean actress, teacher, producer, and director. For ten years she was the Artistic Director of the Shakespeare-by-the-Book Festival. In addition to the fourteen productions she directed for that company, she has directed for The Houston Shakespeare Festival, Summer Shakespeare at Notre Dame, Bucknell University, Houston Community College, and the University of Houston Downtown. She founded and for twenty years was head of the Drama Department at Houston Community College Central College, and on a grant from the National Endowment for the Humanities she was one of 18 teachers selected nationwide to participate in the Folger Shakespeare Library's Teaching Shakespeare through Performance project.